Thursday Night Confessions...

Jana Caldwell

Thursday Night Confessions...

Jana Caldwell

Mockingbird Lane Press

Thursday Night Confessions
Copyright © 2013 Jana Caldwell

Mockingbird Lane Press—Maynard, Arkansas
Library of Congress information in publishing data
ISBN: 978-0-9889542-7-4
0 9 8 7 6 5 4 3 2 1

Mockingbird Lane Press USA
www.mockinbirdlanepress.com
Cover Design by Jamie Johnson
Inside illustrations by Nancy Riney, Maynard, Arkansas

To the Spousal Unit & Child... Mike & Stephanie

Acknowledgements

I have to admit...This whole book idea was a fluke. It's a good feeling when your everyday thoughts and experiences bring people joy and for that I would like to thank everyone that had anything to do with my fluke...

Stanley and Vicki Camp for a support and encouragement that one can only dream of in a job...Krystal Niswonger and Melinda Ochs for always telling me how it is...Cathy Johnson for showing me how things could be...Kathy Rash for showing me the kind of strong woman I aspire to be...Lisa Moore-Miller for the powdered donuts...James Tucker for all his help with my book and teaching me big words...Carol Reynolds, my "stylist" and killer of the "poof"...Jamae and Jeania, my sweet sisters for untying me as a child...Angie Caldwell, my "Go To Girl"...Regina Williams and Jamie Johnson for their long suffering and patience...Andrew Turner for "liking" every status I ever posted...Sweet Treats Bakery for the motivation...The Shults' rooster for the sleepless nights that led to many stories...My clients, family and friends for the material...Strangers—for even better material...And each and every one of my Facebook friends that encouraged me to do this...

Hold Me...

I understand networks and their Christmas themed shows but on The Outdoor Channel—"Hunting Rudolph with Santa," is maybe going a bit too far...

I received an alert yesterday via text from AT&T that my purchase had gone through. Puzzled by this, I asked my son-in-law, the ex-AT&T guy, what I had purchased.

It seems at some point yesterday in my crazy travels, my rear end signed up for mobile email. I can't keep from thinking about that joke where the rear end is so large it formed its own zip code.

I hope it signing up for email is not its first step towards forming a city...

While standing in the checkout line at Wal Mart I discovered everything in my Christmas stocking came from the "impulse buy" section...

Had a conversation with a man earlier about a decision he and his wife were making. His exact words were, "I have 30 years of experience, she has an opinion."

Hmmm...my opinion is he may be experiencing the sofa tonight...

Well...if I want the fru fru coffee without the fru fru price, I can hook up my old coffee maker, make the coffee part with it, pour in a cup, take that cup, put it in my fru fru maker and use the automatic frother and milk adder and do that whistling fancy part that makes you think it will overflow but stops right at the rim of the cup thing...

Then I have my fancy fru fru coffee without the fru fru price.

Of course it is a lengthy process...I may need a cup of coffee first...

On one hand I hope it's not the flu but on the other hand kinda relieved I have something to blame the achy body on other than old age...

I just put my phone in the tube carrier thing at the bank. It is very possible I may need a nap...

No matter how many times you hit the snooze button or flip the little button on the top, your alarm clock will not go off when it is actually your phone ringing...

Trust me on this one...

Okay...I probably need to tell this before someone else does. Misplaced my keys. Looked...looked...looked...no keys. Started backtracking what I did last night. Finally found my keys this morning...

Wrapped up in a Christmas present...

Ok...so in all fairness...if I brought him a lemon square Thursday night and it is still there on Saturday morning...it's fair game, right?

I have found it takes two cups of coffee to get my morning going right. Sadly, the first cup is dedicated to just washing down all the old person pills I have to take and the second is for the caffeine kick...Hold me...

Over the past few days, I have eaten two bags of delicious-delectable-only-here-once-a-year Cadbury Chocolate Mini Eggs, blamed it on my client and really don't feel that bad about it.

Don't judge me...

I got to thinking about Krystal Niswonger hurting herself EXERCISING yesterday.

They sent her to a SPORTS medicine doctor at a SPORTS Wellness Complex, he had all kinds of SPORTS MD certificates on the wall and the guy that fitted her for her brace was from a SPORTS Medical Supply store...

If she had tripped going to the kitchen for a Twinkie, where would they have sent her?

◦ ◦ ◉◉ ◦ ◦

I don't know if something is up with FB or it is just my rugged good looks, but I had 17 friend requests this morning...and they weren't all from naked women in Russia or 20 year old men in Turkey...

They were actual people nearby. This sooooo makes up for all those times in school when I was picked last for dodgeball...

◦ ◦ ◉◉ ◦ ◦

Last night I dreamed I was trying to dry clothes and no matter how long I dried them, they still weren't dry... In essence, I dreamed of a household appliance...

Man...What an exciting life I lead...

I attempted to purchase Build-a-Bear gift cards for my great nieces yesterday...

After waiting in line for 10 minutes while a parent complained about their child's dog, I finally approached the counter.

CASHIER: Welcome to Build-a Bear, will you be making a new friend with us today?

ME: (refraining from making some inappropriate joke) Ummmm...No thank you, I just need a couple of gift cards.

CASHIER: No, problem. Are you a Fluffy Stuff Blah Blah member?

ME: No ma'am, no thank you.

CASHIER: It only takes a second and you receive lots of goodies with it.

ME: I really don't come here a lot.

CASHIER: You might if you had a fluffy stuff card.

ME: blank stare

CASHIER: Okay, which of these gift cards do you want? (holding up a bear one and a logo one)

ME: The bear ones.

CASHIER: Okay...Todd, do you know where the bear cards are? I know they are somewhere. Let me check in the back.

ME: No, just give me 2 of those logo ones.

CASHIER: Are you sure? It won't take long.

ME: My husband has already fallen asleep on the bench outside, I better hurry.

CASHIER: Okay. How much do you want them for?
ME: $20 each.
CASHIER: We have a promotion right now if you spend $30 you get another half price gift card.
ME: Huh?
CASHIER: You could spend $10 more and get double the free gift card that you wouldn't have if you just get the two $20 gift cards.
ME: How much does it cost to make a bear?
CASHIER: $10
ME: Then I'm good with what I have.
CASHIER: Okay...(with attitude) just trying to save you some money.
ME: No you are not...You are draining my soul...
CASHIER: blank stare. Do you want these in a gift box?
ME: Sure, why not?
CASHIER: Here is your purchase ma'am. Have a great day and remember...It's always a great day at Build-a-Bear. (sarcastic smile)
   Well played Build-a-Bear...well played...

⚬ ⚬ ● ◉ ● ⚬ ⚬

We found a lone shingle lying on our porch this morning...

I'm no roofing expert but I'm pretty sure they aren't supposed to be there...

Tis a sad development...

I love how it is perfectly acceptable to have lengthy conversations with total strangers at Wal Mart...

I feel so special...when I get up in the morning...my coffee is made...and hot! All I have to do is pour in my creamer, froth and add the whip cream...I suspect this is how a princess feels...

Has reached the age where she has to take heartburn pills and also apparently the age where she can't remember if she took her heartburn pill or not. Just had lunch...will know shortly, I'm sure.

I'm still slightly freaked for a split second when I'm in another town and someone calls me by name...until I realize I'm wearing a nametag...

On a side note the 2 ladies beside me are having a heated discussion about Joe Biden...I guess me sharing the fact the frosting on my cupcake resembles Elvis wouldn't really impress them, huh? Wrong crowd...

Still not used to my phone and keep taking random pictures of my feet, my client's feet, the sky, my tires, a stranger's rear...I may do a collage...

Little House on the Prairie...it's the one where Pa cries...

No matter how many times I say "I'm going to sleep late!" or how bad I want to, my internal alarm clock wins and I am wide awake at 6 a.m...

Kinda the same way my internal skinny chick says "Go ahead and eat that Krispy Kreme..." Color me wide awake with chocolate sprinkles on my face...

"I don't have a dog in that hunt." My new favorite phrase. Now, if I could just have a situation to use it in. Took me 2 years to fit "Not my first rodeo" into a conversation...

CHRISTMAS DECOR REMOVAL PLAN...
Step 1) Take everything Yuletide related and pile on table...
Step 2) Nap...
Step 3) Stare at tree and mentally plan attack for removal...
Step 4) Nap...
Step 5) Make an Executive decision to postpone removal until a later date...
Step 6) supper...
Step 7) Sit with back to tree to pretend you didn't procrastinate again this year...

I stopped at Atlanta Bread Company to get my sick young-uns some soup. The boy behind the counter suggested baked potato soup as a sure fire remedy for the flu. While his coworker was packing the bag, he asked me if I wanted sour cream in the soup. The cashier said "Dude, NO! My Nana said to never have milk products with the flu." He made me smile. I wonder if Nana knows what a positive effect she had on this young boy's life...

Yesterday on FB we posted a photo of a dog, had 3 people want him and then last night the owner saw him on here and they are being reunited! You can do anything on here! It's like a little city and David Statler is the Court Jester...

· · ○ ◐ ○ · ·

That moment you are lying in bed in between snooze alarms and you hear the rain and thunder and mentally scan your body to see if anything feels bad enough to justify staying there...

· · ○ ◐ ○ · ·

I don't know if you could actually call it "Playing in the snow," but when I slipped on the ice and fell in the snow, I made what resembled a snow angel while trying to get up...a snow angel that no doubt was drunk and had been shot, but nonetheless, a snow angel...

I had a young man ask me this morning via private message if I was a racer.

I replied, "Well, I am trying. I have a big event this morning that the whole town gets involved in! Should be a lot of fun whether I finish or not."

After a second glance, I realized he asked if I was a racist.

I have tried to apologize, but it seems I have been blocked...and I'm sure added to a list somewhere.

Note to self: pick up glasses from the office.

∘ ∘ ◉ ∘ ∘ ∘

Snooze buttons...because people can't do math at six a.m.

∘ ∘ ◉ ∘ ∘ ∘

I woke up at 3 a.m. with the song, "There's something women love about a pickup truck," stuck in my head. Don't judge me...

∘ ∘ ◉ ∘ ∘ ∘

We got a new sofa in the living room and now I feel as if my whole Feng Shui is off...I've even developed a limp and a slight stutter...

I'm not a "cow person," as some of you so eloquently pointed out. I mean I can spot one in a crowd, I do enjoy eating them, wearing their boots and I have stepped in more than my share of cow poo over the years, but no, I don't know what makes them tick.

Night before last I was awakened-awoke-woke up to the sound of one bawling, seemed right outside my window. I thought the neighbor's cow was out. Went to the back deck—couldn't hear it, bathroom window—no cow, front door—none there.

Now look I know what a cow SOUNDS like. I finally give up on my cattle drive and head back to bed only to hear it again...coming from the sleeping Spousal Unit beside me. Okay, so I don't know what a cow SOUNDS like...do they have a night course in "Cattle 101" at BRTC?

∘ ∘ ⊙ ● ⊙ ∘ ∘

So, I'm sleepy at night because I stayed up late the night before, so I turn in early and then wide awake at four a.m., so...I am sleepy at night because I got up early so I turn in early and wide awake at four a.m., so...I am sleepy at night, so I turn in early, blah, blah, blah...for the Love of Santa, let me sleep, man!

As I rounded the corner of mile marker two of the 5k yesterday I was feeling really good. Had the sun on my face and the wind on my back. I could see a group ahead of me...way ahead of me and I could hear a group in the distance behind me.

About that time the little boy on the three wheel thing, I always wanted as a kid, passed me by, giving me a cool nod as he did. Just as he passed a little red headed boy was suddenly at my side. We chatted about school, his siblings and semi trucks.

I asked who his mommy was and he told me her name and added "She is way up there, you probably can't even see her up there she's so far."

And then he was off to join the three wheel boy. I glance to my side and he has been replaced by a little blonde headed boy. He mentioned Legos, horses and big trucks. (I find big trucks to be a common denominator and a sure fire conversation starter with little boys.)

I asked who his mom was and he looked up at me and said "I don't know her name, I call her mom."

I feel we bonded...

Let me get this straight...there is a piece of metal the size of a school bus hurtling toward Earth with a 1 in 3,500 chance it may hit me? Those are better odds than me finding my way home every night...

Dear Subconscious...we need to talk...

The dream you put me in last night was quite a trip. First off, I do appreciate the good memories of my daddy...however, it seems from what I understand I was waiting to go see him? My dad has been gone for 12 years...while I am all for that and do believe I will see him again one day...I'm not quite ready just yet. Sitting in the train station with the guy from the Folgers's commercial was a nice touch but that blonde hussy you added, who was holding my suitcase, was uncalled for in my opinion.

I just wanted to clear that up with you and ask maybe in the future if you could insert George Stephanopoulos into a few more dreams.

Oh...and next time you give my suitcase to that brazen little trollop...make sure she packs my pudding. That is all, Jana...

· ◦ ◌ ◍ ◌ ◦ ·

Dear Dove Body Wash:

While I don't feel "Revived," "Tingly," and like a "New Woman," as your bottle promised, I do find the Pomegranate and Sunflower scent attracts squirrels, baby deer and various other small creatures...and for this...I thank you.

XOXOX Jana

DEAR DRUNKEN GIRL WHO CALLED AT 4:54 a.m.:

I believe you said your name was Jennifer? Well, Jennifer, Honey...first off...yes, the moon was beautiful and I appreciate you pointing that out. We can never see too many moons...secondly...no, there is no Jim at this number, which my outgoing message should have explained...as well as my reply to the follow-up text you sent. Now that this issue is cleared up, I will let you in on a little secret...from many years of trial and error I have learned...you only wake sleeping men if there is a buck in the yard larger than the one he has hanging on the wall, OR if there is an intruder in the house that has actually been spotted and identified as dangerous. I hope this helps for your future calling endeavors and remember Jenny...friends don't let friends dial drunk...

I miss my Drive Thru Girl. My mornings just aren't the same. I would go inside to see if she is working but I'm not sure what constitutes stalking in the Fast Food World...

I just saw where the Hostess workers are on strike and they are predicting it may be the end of Twinkies. This is no way to start the day. Come on folks...can't we all just get along? Hold me...

As I headed to the drive thru yesterday for my tea...no compliment, no sweet gestures, no friendly greeting to start my day...just tea, I had pretty much come to grips with the fact that my marvelous morning ritual had been replaced with "Here's your change."

I took my change and smiled politely and moved ahead to the next window. When it opened it was like chocolate bunnies, fuzzy puppies and Christmas morning all rolled into one...MY girl was back AND apparently promoted to the FRONT window!

She handed me my tea and said, "Here you go honey, You go out and make it a great day!"

I'm not ashamed to admit, I teared up a little. Well done Mickey D's...Well done...

· ◦ ◉●◉ ◦ ·

Had my first Indian food tonight...coincidently...my last too...

· ◦ ◉●◉ ◦ ·

I got up at midnight...seventy-three in the house... kicked on the air...got up at six a.m...sixty-six degrees... kicked on the heat...It's a vicious circle...

Poor ol' Mike was sound asleep and missed all four seasons in an eight hour span at Caldwell Manor...

Everyone has friends that fill certain areas of their lives. You may not see them every day or every week or month but the bond is still there.

That one friend that will give you the advice you may not want but need to hear, the one that lifts your spirits, the one that will loan you that special scarf or the shirt off her back, the one that will be in the hospital with you when you feel all alone, the one that gives you love life advice, the one that will get up in the middle of the night to help move a body...I mean sofa, the one that listens to you as you cry yourself to sleep and the one that sees you for you and still loves you.

But lastly I don't want to forget the one that tells you how it is. The one that reads your post about being warped and simply tells you..."You aren't screwed up, you're just terribly broken...but repairable..."

Bless you one and all...

Okay, so they are doing away with Twinkies and Ding Dongs but we are gaining a new product called "CRACKER JACK."

Our childhood popcorn snack souped up with caffeine...

I wonder what the much anticipated prize inside will be...those tiny bottles of airplane liquor or maybe a crack pipe in a variety of cool colors?

I swear folks...is nothing sacred?

I try to keep upbeat on here and seldom have bad days; some may be trying and stressful and sometimes I may milk the situation for a little attention (just my nature) but for the most part, I'm healthy, happy and have my share of blessings in my life.

I have an amazing husband, children, family and friends too numerous to count. Yesterday however, was one of the most difficult days I have ever had. Dealing with an aging parent is sometimes overwhelming. I found myself sitting alone in an office, waiting on a meeting with her doctor and listening/overhearing...okay, eaves-dropping on a conversation going on in the hall.

The gentleman was telling a story about his mother. I missed the bulk of the conversation but did hear him say..."Well, then she started dating a man that had a pet chimpanzee. I never liked him."

I smiled a small smile for the first time that day and thought to myself...Okay, things could be worse...and then I had the undying urge to ask if it was the man he didn't like or the chimp? I am so incredibly warped; it is a miracle I can function in everyday life...

My Holly Jolly Spirit gets really off balance when I see people mowing their lawn in shorts and flip flops under the shadow of their 8 foot Frosty and Flashing Rudolph...

Sitting in the book store listening to four little girls talk about where babies come from...

The eldest and apparently the leader of the pack told the others, "My mom swallowed the baby so it can grow and then in about a year she poops it out."

This was followed by "Ewwwwwww" from the remaining three.

I feel they need to hear the truth, but I don't want to ruin their Christmas and I spent my bail money on new boots...

Well I finished the first book I have read in 30 years and have experienced every emotion imaginable in doing so. I am generally "watch the movie" kinda gal, but reading is so much more intense. I don't remember *White Fang* affecting me this way...

Pondering one of life's little mysteries...why do you go to Paula Dean's Buffett and eat a salad? Seriously man...you have a plate full of lettuce and there are crab legs up there...I can't even look at you...

As we stepped into Toys R Us last night looking around, a loud young boy, maybe 10ish, from a few aisles over, was catching everyone's attention. He was continually complaining about the store not having what he wanted and arguing with everyone and just in a general loud, hateful bad mood.

What I assume to be his mother or warden or some adult figure, escorting the beast, tried to calm him by agreeing with every snide remark the little angel made towards the store and its employees.

As they finally made it to the front of the store and headed out the door, my dear sweet Melinda smiling towards the family said, "Yeah, that kid's gonna get beat up a few times in his life..." then casually went on with her shopping.

I don't think I have ever been so proud of her in my life...

• ○ ◐ ● ◑ ○ •

TODAY I LEARNED:

1) You can fashion a cooler out of the hotel trash can if needed for pool side.

2) Just because you can wear a bikini, doesn't mean you should...

As I stepped onto the elevator with the ninety plus year old, very well dressed man in a wheelchair, I smiled and said, "Hi."

He said "Well, hello there Sweetheart, how was your night?"

I told him I had a good night and was headed to my room.

"Why don't you come on up to my room and see what kind of trouble we can get into," he grinned and winked.

I raised my eyebrow and glanced at what I assumed to be his nurse and she just smiled and shook her head as if she was used to this.

I smiled and said, "Well, I tell you what...when that door opens I will race you to the end of that hall and we will see if you can keep up with me."

He took my hand and kissed it and said, "Oh honey, you just made an old man's day."

Then he looked at his nurse and said "Laura, hold my wine and unhook my oxygen...I've got a race to win...

Slightly freaked out when I walked in bathroom to see one of my bath mats covered in blood...until I realized it wasn't blood, but the blush that I spilled this morning. Age + Memory Loss + Bad eyesight = other bath mat wet now...

That awkward moment when shopping and you run into a client who casually checks out your cart and asks "What's for dinner?" only to find Preparation H and feminine products...

· ○ ◐ ● ◑ ○ ·

I may cringe at the site of a spider; run over a client when I see a snake and even wet myself when confronted by a state trooper while carrying a gun...I admit I'm a pansy...

BUT...it takes a pretty tough woman to have lava hot wax spread on her lip and ripped off like an old Band-Aid and NOT shed a tear...just sayin...

I am woman, hear me roar...

· ○ ◐ ● ◑ ○ ·

The girl that just waited on me had vampire teeth. The service "sucked" but I'm a little afraid to snub her...

· ○ ◐ ● ◑ ○ ·

My computer just flashed MEMORY DUMP and rebooted. Can't really see where this could be a good thing...

As I was driving home yesterday...pondering...it occurred to me if the world falls apart and we drop "off the grid," I am not prepared. I have no cash on hand...should probably bury some in the yard. I wonder if cash will even be worth anything then...Mike reloads so we will have ammo and can barter with that, I guess. I may need to acquire a few chickens and a pig to trade because I doubt we can get much from a Demon Cat trade, plus I'm sure we would eat him first.

On second thought, I'm eating the Shults' rooster first. It's just the natural cycle, man. I probably need to stock up on coffee and bacon. They always had bacon in the olden days. This may require a place to keep cold stuff...we can dig a hole...okay, Mike can dig a hole. I only have 1 fruit tree but I have 5 pepper plants, which I am sure will bring up a whole new issue living on peppers... I'm afraid this will have a very adverse affect/effect on my poof...and ice cream. Hold me...

Watching the guy walk across Niagara Falls...twenty stories up and they are asking him questions...

"You look like you are enjoying this Nick."

"Are the bugs bothering you?"

Really? Let me question the crazy man...

"So, how close are you to wetting yourself, Nick?"

I am contemplating reading...I may go as far as purchasing a book....of course, then I fear if I read I will have to purchase glasses...maybe I can just sit with my coffee and un-purchased book and un-purchased glasses in my happy place with all the pretty people...

They shall never know my secret...

A man followed me out of Wal Mart and asked me if I wanted to go out for a steak. As I drove off thinking... Yeah, I still got it! It occurred to me...

What made him approach me with the promise of food as opposed to a movie or dancing...

I guess it's all about reading your target audience...

I just met a woman who has a twenty-two-year-old, twenty-one-year-old, a fifteen, fourteen and thirteen-year-old and a baby; with probably the most arrogant, sexist husband I have ever had the displeasure of meeting.

My guess is she spent most of the 90's intoxicated...

Does it sadden anyone else that Twisted Sister is doing a Stanley Steamer commercial? It just ruins their bad boy image for me...

It would be like Samuel L. Jackson doing a softer side iphone commercial...

Oh wait...

I have an overwhelming fear of driving off from the gas pump with the nozzle still attached in my tank. Overwhelming as in I look back at tank, look at pump and look in mirror as I drive off just to be sure...

Do they have therapy or meetings for this disorder... maybe a gum?

On my way back to reality this morning with just one question...This wing of the Hotel has like 20 rooms, every morning so far I have noticed they put newspapers in front of like 3...mine being one of them. How do they decide who needs to keep up with what's going on in the world and whom did I speak to that put me on the list? I do not recall any political questions upon check in...

I'm starting to tire and sweat...not a good combination for a woman of my age and size...at a party of 100 and know maybe 6...

I've dozed off twice, listened to at least a dozen Arkansas jokes and introduced myself as Fern, Uncle Joe's cousin more times than I know...

Someone please...make it rain.

· ○ ◉●◉ ○ ·

As I leaned over...in my bathrobe...to put the empty tray in the hallway, I had no idea how heavy the door was...I was to quickly find out it was heavy enough to slam into my derriere, catapult me into the hallway and quickly slam behind me...

Did I mention...IN MY BATHROBE?

No key, no phone, on the 14th floor and yes...in my bathrobe, I make my way to the lobby phone nodding at oncoming guests as if I was just out for a morning stroll... Exactly 7 minutes after the initial lock out, I was kindly let back in my room by a sweet boy I will call Phileppe...

NOTE TO SELF: Put extra key in robe pocket...just in case...

That is all...

I just realized I am wearing a wishbone necklace and bird earrings. I'm sure that breaks some sort of fashion rule...

And at least nine kinds of poultry rules...

The lady in the box just told me due to upcoming traffic delays that I will be 8 minutes late. How? I feel the lady in the box knows too much...

There is a Starbucks in the lobby and a young man named Brad that carries our bags and sends milk and cookies to our room because "we've had a long day."

Please forward mine and Melinda's mail and water our plants. We are never leaving...

After trying on no less than 112 swimsuits, I have made an executive decision to bring back cutoffs and t-shirts...anyone with me?

That awkward moment when you realize it IS a toupee and then you realize you've stared way too long...

My broker cleaned off his desk last night and found $23, the missing surface-to-air missiles and a small child...

I aspire to be like him...

⚬ ◦ ● ◉ ○ ◦ ⚬

Found myself in Wal Mart yesterday with what appeared to be a small army or chain gang of tiny children...screaming, pushing, biting, yelling, and yes, even a few curse words came out of the group.

Got to me thinking...the witch from *Hansel and Gretel* was totally misunderstood...

⚬ ◦ ● ◉ ○ ◦ ⚬

I have come to the conclusion that I hate getting ready in the morning. Yes, the shower is refreshing, but then you shave, shampoo, rinse, repeat, lotion up, mousse, blow dry, poof, spray, make-up, and on and on.

I suspect when the showers and such are no longer a must-do for my line of work, I will become a stinky old person that you must force to bathe and is covered in cat hair from my seventy-two furry friends.

⚬ ◦ ● ◉ ○ ◦ ⚬

I'm more of a "touch the fire to know it's hot" kinda girl...

Cell block 6...Female lockup on TV and drinking Nyquil...throw in some pork rinds and I feel the start of a new Christmas Tradition...

∘ ∘ ◉ ⦿ ◉ ∘ ∘

I saw a man carrying his wife effortlessly across their yard this morning, then I saw a man climbing a tree with a running chainsaw and just now James operated on our printer with a Buck knife...I feel very "Me Tarzan, You Jane" today.

∘ ∘ ◉ ⦿ ◉ ∘ ∘

I can make it from my bed, across the bedroom, into the bathroom and back to bed, semi-awake, pretty much every night.

Last night, I made it out of my bed, across the bedroom, living room, dining room and kitchen to the mudroom before I woke up.

I can only assume I was headed for the litter box...

∘ ∘ ◉ ⦿ ◉ ∘ ∘

At the Game & Fish Commission in Little Rock waiting...people watching...whole different breed of folk down here...they have a gift shop, think you get a free t-shirt with every easement?

Saturday when we were at the movie, they were showing the preview for that one called *Mama*.

I had my hands over my face, of course, but when the preview was over and the theater went black...

About 3 rows back a little kid said "Mama..."

It was priceless! Very cool moment that might have scared a lesser woman. The fact that I dug in my nails to the point of bringing blood to Mike's hand and wet myself was sheer coincidence, I'm sure.

After a trying morning yesterday, I momentarily escaped the turmoil to try and spread some love and joy around town. I was standing in the bakery drooling when one of the owners came through the front door grinning from ear to ear and said, "You know what makes me happy? Sir-Mix-A Lot makes me happy!"

I looked at her questioningly and said, "Sir-Mix-A-Lot?"

This prompted both owners to start dancing and singing, *"I like big butts and I cannot lie!"*

On one hand, I was really hoping my appearance didn't provoke them serenading me...but on the other hand, does anyone else find it humorous that a bakery's theme song is about oversized derrieres?

Went shopping yesterday evening at the mall...I was putting my stuff in the Jeep when I saw a fight in front of Barnes and Noble. It was 3 teenagers. I had my phone in my hand and walked over right in the middle of them and said, "TURN HIM LOOSE OR I'M GOING TO CALL YOUR MOM."

The kid let him go and started stuttering out excuses. I turned and walked away...Amateurs...

                        ⚬ ⚬⚬●⚬ ⚬ ⚬

I was just given some advice...if someone breaks into your house...the police don't need to interview 2 people...

                        ⚬ ⚬⚬●⚬ ⚬ ⚬

This man on TV was missing for seventy-six days and no one looked for him...

Okay folks...if you, at any time, don't hear from me for like two hours tops...please send help...

                        ⚬ ⚬⚬●⚬ ⚬ ⚬

I have never been so glad to be home...except that time I got food poisoning and drove 12 hours straight back from Texas—was pretty stoked then too—but this rates up there...

Yesterday I went into Price Chopper for one glazed donut. Yes, just one. They were sold out of the single donuts, but had a box of a dozen packed up. The lady "suggested" I just get that.

Well, made sense to me. At this point I thought, I needed some yogurt...to offset the donuts, so I headed to the back of the store. On my way to the back, I passed Cracker Jacks and had a childhood flashback moment, so I grabbed a bag. Wondering if the prize is as fun as back then. Just past those they had the white chocolate peppermint pretzels that you NEVER see, so I grabbed a bag...then two more.

At this point, it was a balancing act, but I prevailed and headed on back toward the yogurt. The upcoming Nyquil on my left just spoke to me...I had to partake and grabbed a bottle. It is medicine, you know "cough—cough."

Past the Little Debbies, past the Oreos, past the Nacho Cheese Doritos (all of which I declined) and finally to the yogurt.

Well, I should get plenty since I'm here...they are awfully small, I thought. So I picked up five peach and one strawberry and headed back to the register.

Then, Oh! The dollar aisle...Mike is out of aspirin, so I grabbed him two bottles, Oh! Cat treats for a dollar, grabbed the furry friends a package...

Then proceeded to the cashier and unloaded all my must haves. Twenty minutes, twenty-seven dollars and four bags later, I headed to my car...with my one donut.

Never. Shop. Hungry.

One of my good friends is an author, librarian and overall book nut. Any time I am out shopping and come across a book signing, I buy her the autographed book because she collects them.

One day I was in a bookstore in St. Louis and there was an author signing her new release. I picked up the book, not paying any attention to the content and stood in line waiting my turn with several other women.

When it was my turn, the author asked me who it was for. I told her it was for my girlfriend, Debbie Archer.

She smiled, wrote a nice greeting and handed me the book. When I turned to leave, the entire group of people there started clapping and one even said, "Good for you!" I was thinking, Cool, they're thrilled I bought the book and went on with my shopping.

A few days later when I gave my friend the book, I told her the story of how happy they were that I bought the book for her. She started reading the back, which I had not, and proceeded to crack up.

Seems this was a love story of two women that longed to be together, but due to a "narrow-minded society," they just couldn't be.

Ahhhhhh...makes sense now...

I really do feel the big hair offsets the big hips...

Went thru the drive thru at Hardee's in Timbuckto and ordered a roast beef sandwich. The guy told me they haven't had roast beef in 5 years and that I really need to get out more...

· ○ ◉●◉ ○ ·

I see all these landmarks, buildings, etc. named after people and I hope one day to do something great enough to have something named after me...maybe a highway, a hospital, a sandwich...

· ○ ◉●◉ ○ ·

ON THE HATFIELDS & MCCOYS...

Sitting with my coffee, taking a moment to ponder all the blessings...the air is cold...the coffee is hot...I have the good creamer...my daughter is in love...the spider that made me wet myself is dead...the Spousal Unit is a wonderful-wonderful man...business is good...rain is coming and Kevin Costner declared the feud is over...

Color me a happy camper.

· ○ ◉●◉ ○ ·

Last night when Johnsee had to choose between staying in the Hatfield family or marrying Roseanna...he looked at her, then he looked at his dad, and then he looked back at her...

Mike said, "He hesitated...he hesitated too long. Now, you know, no matter what he does in the future, she will always bring that up when they argue..."

You would have thought by Episode 2 that the Hatfield's would have learned not to invite the McCoy's to picnics...

I was watching Hatfields and McCoys last night and when Johnsee Hatfield romanced Roseanna McCoy and then the brothers shot him...I was glued to the TV and The Spousal Unit was reading a gun magazine...he heard gunfire (which caught his attention) and I gasped and said, "They shot Johnsee!"

Mike, trying to keep up, asked, "They shot the baby daddy?" Ummmm...

What the heck has he been watching?

I haven't figured out if he is a Hatfield or a McCoy but I'm on Kevin Costner's side...

Sometimes...in the morning...I will shave my right leg first instead of my left leg...just to shake things up a little...

Wildside, I know...But that's just how I roll...

· ∘ ● 🌑 ● ∘ ·

I was awakened from a deep slumber at 6 a.m. by my "surprise" automatic coffee maker that sounded like a spaceship going off on the kitchen counter...Tuesday tucked tail and hit the closet, Demon Cat dropped The Baby Jesus and I'm not sure but I might have wet myself just a little...

· ∘ ● 🌑 ● ∘ ·

Listening to a man discipline his child...very calmly...

"Okay son, you have two choices, Do you want my left foot up your butt, or my right? I can go either way with it. I believe a man needs choices in his life."

As of five minutes ago, the son has yet to decide...

· ∘ ● 🌑 ● ∘ ·

I figured out yesterday after running home to pick something up that in "Music Time" it only takes me a *Back in Black* and *Carefree Highway* to get home...

Good commute.

THINGS I LEARNED WHILE RINGING THE SALVATION ARMY BELL...

1) People will pay you to stop—especially if they are on the phone.
2) Various cats live at Wal Mart—they do NOT like to be petted.
3) The food entrance is where the big bucks are—I shall set my sights on that end.
4) There is a backup bell—wonder what happened to provoke that.
5) They quit ringing at eight—at least that's when a man in a red shirt came and took my bucket & bell—maybe I should have asked for ID...

Reflecting back on one of the busiest weeks this year with a blessed week at work, numerous parties with great friends, my sweet daughter and her hubby home and just all the hustle and bustle of the holiday's creeping in...and the one thing that stands out through all the craziness... there is absolutely no lady like way to eat hot wings...

The airbag light in my passenger side seat showed it was automatically turned off sensing a small child was in it. It was my purse...

WHAT I LEARNED AT 3:34 a.m...

While getting a drink in the kitchen in pitch black, if you stand right in front of the sink, slightly lean back and look out the front window...the neighbors vapor light looks like a giant shining star on top of our Christmas Tree...

. . . .

I'm drinking cocoa from a Christmas Mug and looking at a naked tree...I feel festive...also I can't remember the last time I played pinball...I miss pinball...

. . . .

I have not only reached the point in my life that I have to wear glasses, I have also reached the point I search and search for them just to find they were on my head...
Hold me...

. . . .

I have a big head, physically, not mentally...I sadly noticed that today...

. . . .

I feel remarkably good and clear headed for being up since two a.m...Elvis, please pass John the turnips...Thank you, thank you very much...

I was at a party earlier this week and received a pleasant surprise. My McDonalds Drive Thru Girl I love so much was the entertainment! It seems not only does she make strangers feel special with her cheery spirit but this girl can sing!! Very impressive! I went up and introduced myself and told her what a joy she brings to my morning and then I swallowed hard and asked her..."Do you remember me?" I wanted to know if I was special or just a face in the crowd to her and you know what she said?

"I remember your hair..."

I couldn't contain my excitement...I smiled really big and hugged her hard...SHE DOES REMEMBER ME!!!...I expect the restraining order at anytime...

Great advancements in Operation Christmas Decor tonight...I have successfully moved the two tubs of decorations from the closet to the living room floor...I'm trying to pace myself...

Watching a news clip about a man that turned out to be a serial killer...his neighbor said he was always an odd man....said he would kill squirrels......AND EAT THEM!! Who knew?

My thought process at three a.m. I wake up to go to the restroom and notice my tongue is numb. Wait...tongue numb? Isn't that a sign of anaphylactic shock? It must be the cough medicine I took. I'm allergic to the cough medicine I took. It didn't work anyway, I have coughed all night, and now it's going to kill me...no wait...it's not numb tongue, its swollen tongue. Okay, it's not swollen. I'm good. Of course, the cough medicine still didn't work and why is my tongue numb? Do tongues go to sleep like your feet do? Hehehe...my tongue was sleeping while I was. Actually, it makes sense. Why do more people not speak of this...cat got their tongue...hehehe...cat got their numb tongue...Here kitty, kitty, kitty...

I suspect this was "thought overload" from five hours of not thinking...why do more people not speak of this??

* * *

I did my good deed for the day. I helped a little old man with a walker into the bathroom...he was very appreciative...however, the man at the urinal was less than enthused...they really need to put walls around those things... just sayin'...

As I opened the door to my Jeep, a familiar sound rang through the parking lot of Wal Mart. BAM-BAM-BAM-BAM-BAM...

For a split second I had a flashback to The Spousal Unit shooting in the back yard and wasn't alarmed...

Then it hit me where I was and I went into survival mode. First I scoured the parking lot for my child and Kyle and spotted them at the front door.

Good, I thought, they are out of harm's way. I was talking on the phone so I had "Tell Someone" covered. I kept my cool and using my door as a shield I stepped out to locate the source of this sound. As my "cat like" reflexes kicked in, I honed in on the shots coming from the van 2 parking spots over.

BAM-BAM. I crouched down, phone in hand, child in sight and waited for more activity. Just then, a probably seven-to-eight-year-old boy jumps out of the van with his pink toy gun and aimed it directly at what I assume to be the birth mother of this demon spawn.

While in the back of my head I was shouting, Shoot her...shoot her, I was extremely glad it wasn't a real gun scenario and super relieved I had not gone into my next survival step of hitting the ground face down and covering my head...

I awakened the other morning to an excruciating pain in my thigh. In the next fifteen minutes, I would convince myself it was a blood clot in my femoral artery and that when I got up to move around and have my coffee, it would dislodge from its resting place, go to my heart and that would be the end. I had planned what I should wear for the ambulance ride, tell Mike where the bill payment notebook is, text my child that when cleaning out the closet, I found a Christmas present I had hid for her and, just in case, discuss how I wanted my hair done for the photos...because yes...there will be photos. I also mentally planned a really cool newspaper real estate marketing ad for our listings and thought about how to do a clown's makeup to make it a little less scary for adults because let's face it...those things are freaky. I'm a complex woman...

· ○ ◍ ● ◍ ○ ·

Things I'm pondering while lying here unable to move...how hard would it be to fashion some sort of poking device to push the button on the coffee maker and maybe the device double to poke Mike when he snores....why do I feel as if Demon Cat is circling his prey every time he passes by....and exactly how hard would it be to pee in a water bottle flat on your back...

The policeman that just came in and made an offer on the home I showed him Saturday was carrying a pink diaper bag on his shoulder...it was balanced out very well by the firearm on his hip...

Just FYI...
When being pulled over for speeding, saying..."I'm sorry sir, I didn't want to be late for my heart doctor appointment," does get you off with a warning...

I texted my broker with one hand while blow drying my hair with the other...I feel as if I have reached a higher more efficient level of womanism...

So...do I tell the lady beside me she has a noodle stuck to her face or just let it go...I never know my place in situations like this...

Wondering how I can remember lyrics to a song I haven't heard since 1986. But can't, even for a million bucks; remember why I just walked into the kitchen...

Pondering on a wonderful night full of good friends, good food, good stories and good times. One of the most touching, heartwarming, true friendship moments was when we all shared a "blue drink" together. Passed it around the table each taking a drink much like young Indian hunters with their first kill, sharing the animal's heart to signify their upcoming journey through life...

As we shared this drink...one by one...all these amazing, successful women, in all different stages of life, one overwhelming thought stuck in my mind...

There is no telling what I'm going to catch from them. Seriously...feel my head, do I have a fever? Hold me...

⋅　⋅　∘　⦾　◉　◑　∘　⋄　⋅　⋅　⋅

The other night I ordered takeout and when I looked in the bag, I saw they had included four sets of plastic silverware. In other words, someone at the restaurant packed my order, took a second to think about it, and then estimated that there must be at least four people eating to require such a large amount of food.

Too bad I was eating by myself...

I was in Wal Mart when I saw a young couple headed to the "Womanly Product Wall"... (Yes, we have a whole wall). Anyway, the guy stopped dead in his tracks and said, "I will just wait for you by the cart."

The girl walked up, grabbed his hand and said, "NO! You will be a part of this like we talked about!"

He held his ground and said, "No, I will wait here."

She crossed her arms and gave him "The Look."

I was standing there thinking...oh you naive little man...pick your battles sweetie, pick your battles...

On the bright side...the lizard I laid on while sunning probably won't have anything worse happen to him today...and I learned...with proper motivation and correct height and speed...I CAN fly off the back deck.

I see all these pics of girls on TV all skinny and tanned in their swimsuits and I remember "back in the day," I looked like that. But OMG, the maintenance was so time consuming. There was plucking and starving and stressing and grooming and all the wardrobe changes and do these shoes match this shirt...blah, blah, blah...

Geez...things are so much simpler now that I only have two pair of jeans that fit and I can't see my feet...

Sometimes I like to pretend I am Queen of the Universe and you are all my subjects...George...bring Mama some coffee...

. . ●●○ . .

Okay...so the River Monsters guy looks all over the world for fish that "bite back" and catches them...
That sum it up?
Riveting...

. . ●●○ . .

I have several boxes of "stuff" in my closet that I really didn't know what to do with or told myself I would sort later. Today, I have come to the realization that I have no intention of sorting through those boxes...ever. I feel somewhat relieved to let myself off the hook like that.
I think I will nap now.

. . ●●○ . .

I got my lip waxed and then got a milkshake. I'd call it even.

Went to visit an elderly gentleman yesterday whose seventy-year-old "trophy" wife recently left him for an older man she met on FB.

I walked in to visit with a big smile and homemade cookies.

He looked at me and said, "You brought me cookies? I don't need no damn cookies. Why didn't you bring me whiskey?"

I decided to refrain from asking how he is doing since the divorce...

· ● ○ ○ ◉ ○ ○ ·

I called a local business yesterday and as soon as they answered the phone and heard my voice, they started cracking up and said, "It's Jana," laughing uncontrollably then followed with, "I can't believe it's you. We were just talking about you," followed by more laughter.

Well, laughter is contagious, so at this point I'm quite engulfed in my own little laughing spell and said, "What were you talking about?"

HER: "Well, two of us just had our yearly gynecologist appointments and we thought of you."

ME: Silence

It's times like this you can see your true impact on society...

Comment to publisher: Is this to discuss details of a book, or to break it to me in person you aren't interested? I feel like I'm dating...

* ∘ ◐ ● ◑ ∘ *

I was wandering around in a book store and decided to look for something to read in my down time. I headed to the fiction area and was greeted by an employee. I picked up a book I had been eyeing off one of the end cap displays and asked if she knew if this was one in a series. I wasn't going to fall for that again like I did with the last book I read. I get to the end and it wasn't over...then...he says on the last page, LOOK FOR GIDEON AND AVA IN MY NEW BOOK... COMING IN THE FALL.

That was just cruel. Anyway...the employee took the book from me, looked at the back of it and handed it back saying, "I'm sorry, I don't read fiction."

I stood there feeling somewhat scolded for my choice and thought...what are you, 18? Give it 30 more years, 3 kids arguing with you over 12 different issues, a full time job, a spare tire and a stack of bills to pay and you WILL read fiction just for a little escape now and then...Miss Judgmental!!

Sometimes I feel it best I avoid the public while weaning myself off coffee...

Just went down Candy Cane Lane at night for the first time! It is sooooo pretty and lit up bright...except for the one house that I have for sale. Someone really needs to buy it and put up some lights! Santa would want it that way...

Last night our waitress walked up to our table while we were eating, stuck her rear end in our face and asked if she had something on it.

While I'm all about helping a girl out, I found it somewhat inappropriate, so I said, "Yes, yes you do."

Then for the next ten minute we watched her turn around and around in circles like a puppy chasing its tail.

Ahhh...dinner and a show. Next time I'm bringing a ball and a squeeze toy.

Come on princess, ask me again...

I was talking to a man that had recently had a stroke. He asked me to go slow and be patient with him. I was trying to talk slow and articulate.

We'd been talking about 10 minutes when he said, "Jana..."

I said, "Yes sir?"

Then he said, "I lost half my brain, not my hearing."

He apparently didn't lose his sense of humor either...

As I lie in my hotel bed eating my Skittles and watching Rookie Blues, I wasn't startled when I heard the door opening because I expected Steph back at any time.

I glanced over to greet her and was, however, extremely startled to see it wasn't her, but a middle age blonde woman backing in the door with several suitcases.

I didn't know this woman, but she apparently planned on staying awhile. She turned around...and screamed which in turn prompted my scream and the shower of Skittles all over the white comforter.

For a split second I pondered a "Taste the Rainbow" joke but quickly went back to the matter at hand. As we calmed the situation and concluded a mistake had been made at the front desk, I realized the importance of those silver lock thingys at the top of hotel room doors...

But more crucial to the situation I also realized the importance of pants...

I saw a show last night where the girls were wearing shorts with cowboy boots and it was so cute...I feel however, the window for me wearing that ensemble in public has closed...since I'm not 18 or in a Trace Adkins video...

I was in the dressing room at Dillard's yesterday trying on the "end of the summer sale" swimsuits. I heard a baby crying loudly from 2 doors down and then the sales lady come in and knocked on the door.

About that time I was ready to look in the dreaded triple mirror at the end of the hall, so I stepped out of my dressing room. The woman with the baby opened the door and the saleslady asked if she could hold the baby while the mom tried on clothes. She said yes, but the baby had to see her or would throw a fit. The sales lady took the baby and the woman continued to try on clothes with her door open.

About that time a very pretty blonde with a newborn came in the hall and asked if we minded if she breast fed there out of the public view. Of course we didn't so she proceeded. As if on cue, the older lady in the last dressing room stepped out in just her pants and bra and was discussing the size shirt she needed with another sales lady that had joined the group.

So there we all stood, Saleslady with baby, mom with eye on baby, older woman in bra, breast feeding blonde, other sales lady and me in my swimsuit...

All eyes turned to me and every one of them gave their opinion, positive of course, about how great I looked and how it made me look slimmer etc.

I had a mirror...granted I didn't look hideous but I was no Barbie. It was at that moment I smiled and realized...no matter the stage in life a woman is in, they ALL know how important it is to give positive feedback and encouragement when a woman is in the vulnerable position of trying on swimsuits ...

I was trying on dresses when I ran into a couple, about my age, shopping for lingerie. Everything she picked out, he said, "No," and everything he picked out was mainly for eighteen-year-old stick figure models and she wasn't comfortable, so she said "No."

About the tenth piece of dental floss he picked out for her to wear and she vetoed, he said, "If I buy this, you WILL wear it.

Oh no, he didn't. (Insert head bob, shaking finger and hand on hip.) I guess the look on my face and the others around, who up until now had been quietly eavesdropping, made him uncomfortable, so he put the garment, which can only be described as the equivalent to a bedazzled eye patch back on the rack and retreated to another section.

I'm not saying we made a major difference in this man's life, that we made him show some respect for his and all other women, but I'm proud to say, before he left, he looked at me and said, "Your dress looks like a tent."

That's a compliment, right?

My Tassimo wouldn't brew this morning. After a slight panic attack and debating on if this was important enough to wake The Spousal Unit, it hit me..."Owner's Manual." After searching eighteen minutes through numerous gun manuals, appliance papers and one birth certificate I really need to question Mike about, I finally found the fifty-nine page booklet which held the key to a peaceful morning for me, and whether they realize it or not, for many others as well.

God bless the woman that came up with the "Trouble-shooting" section so people with ADD can fix things too.

Of course, the troubleshooting info doesn't use regular words like "the green button on the right," it uses technical terms, which in turn I have to look up in the GLOSSARY. (Look, Tom Towell, I said GLOSSARY. I used something I learned in high school. I always knew listening to you would come in handy and for this...I thank you.) After the GLOSSARY explained there was this thing called a "Manual Button," I was home free. I pushed it and the delectable black gold came pouring out and saved the day. Cheers to you and your GLOSSARY of terms, Mr. Towell...Cheers to you...

As I wandered through the house, not pilfering through things, waiting on Carol to get ready for the Gala, I was startled by a noise coming from the back room. I was puzzled by this, having just left her to get dressed. It was similar to what I suspect a hyena giving birth would sound like.

Now I've seen those horror movies where the unsuspecting friend goes toward the noise and it never ends, well, so everything in my being was saying, "Don't go, don't go, but alas, I couldn't stay away. As I approached the door, I searched the room for some type of weapon and grabbed an ugly flower arrangement in the hall. Hideous, I tell you. A part of me hoped I needed a weapon so we could finally be rid of that awful thing...

Anyway, weapon in hand, I slowly opened the door and what I saw will be burned in my memory for eternity...

It was Carol, dear sweet, skinny Carol, trying to stuff herself into a Spanx. I still today can't get the image from my mind. Poor thing had worked herself into a sweat and was taking a break. I can't describe how she looked lying there so helpless, except...do you remember that scene from *A Christmas Story* where Ralphie's little brother was pushed in the snow with all those layers of coats on and was lying there helpless, trying to get up? Poor thing...looked like a turtle on its back trying to get turned over. Okay, maybe I can describe it.

Anyway, by this time she was ready for her second attempt. I patted her forehead with a damp towel, fixed her a cold drink and gave her *The Little Engine That Could* pep talk and retreated to the hall. I have never had more respect for that woman in my life...

I AM WOMAN; HEAR ME ROAR...Literally...

CALLER: Hey, is this Jana?

ME: Yes.

CALLER: This is Josh XXXX.

ME: Can I help you?

CALLER: Do you remember me?

ME: Ummm, No? Sorry.

CALLER: Don't you work on a Riverboat?

ME: No,   I'm a real estate agent.

CALLER: Okay. Sorry, I must have the wrong Jana.

ME: No problem.
            Hangs up.
            Phone rings again.

CALLER: Jana, I'm sorry. Josh got my phone and called
            the wrong person.

ME: Okay, who is this?

CALLER: This is Tick.

ME: Your name is Tick?

CALLER: Well, it's my nickname.

ME: Do I know you?

CALLER: Well, I thought you did. Where are you from?
            Do you work on the boats?

ME: Do you or your friend need any real estate?

CALLER: Well, no.

ME: Well, I think you have the wrong Jana then.

Riverboat Jana must lead an exciting life...

Odd-ventures in

Real Estate...

All in all I am a pleasant person. I get along with most everyone. I mean there are a few people I won't be Christmas shopping with but I'd pull them in the life raft if our ship sank.

I do get a bit snippy when I get groped by a little boy or someone eats my last piece of chocolate but for the most part I am nice.

Well yesterday I was confronted with a woman that tested that life raft scenario. I was just sitting in the office...polishing my halo...when a man and woman walked in. I stood to greet them and I could tell from the moment this woman opened her mouth, we would NOT be shopping together. She was looking for someone and when I didn't answer her questions to suit her, she as much as called me a liar. This provoked a little sarcasm on my part. She then proceeded to insult me.

Hmmmm... The sarcasm usually shuts them down. I then put into play the hands on the hips maneuver and attempted that head bob thing I have never really mastered and I'm sure knocked me down the ladder a few notches in her eyes.

At this point, as she was still mouthing, I went with the old standby of shaking my finger in her face and talking louder than her. This seemed to work. She tucked her horns back in and headed for the front door. It took all my being not to say, "And don't let the door hit you in the rear on the way out," or "Yeah, and the horse you rode in on!" but I took the high road and kept my silence...

I was really glad this didn't escalate any farther but in the back of my mind I had already planned my defense. I was going to take out the old guy first and use his cane to trip her as I ran... It is always good to have a "Plan B"...

. . .●. . .

Waiting on my 12:00 appointment pondering...I have owned my Jeep for six years and just today found my CD player has a thing called RANDOM TRACK...a magical addition to my listening pleasure...now...does anyone know how the heck to get it off RANDOM TRACK?

. . .●. . .

I realize ten acres is not a lot to walk, but when you walk EVERY INCH of it, it is. About an acre in, I realized—I had to pee, three acres...ate too much at Christmas, five acres...my socks bunched up in my boots, six acres...considered a different career, eight acres...never walk with your hands in your pockets on rocks...ouch, nine acres...thought I saw Elvis. But after ten acres I heard the sweetest words a man can say...
"Where do I sign?"

As I stepped out of my Jeep I could feel their eyes upon me. They were grouped together off to the side...what seemed to be at least a dozen kids...which I soon discovered were just three. But these three were diabolical. I shook hands with the parents and made my way to the front door...somewhat cautiously.

No sooner had the little one stepped on the porch; he made his way up and did what can only be described as "latched" himself to me.

I made eye contact with Mama, with what I can only imagine was the same look that deer on the highway gets as the car tops the hill.

She waved her hand at me and said, "Oh...he's a friendly little one."

All righty then, this was normal. I went on to show the home, dragging "little one" along like a gimp leg. I broke free from him when they made their way up the stairs. Relief was mine. That relief was short-lived when "little one" appeared again. He circled around like a wild cat does his prey.

I had nowhere to hide...it was like he was on a mission and at me he came...planting his head right smack in the middle of my chest and wrapping his hands around me until he was gripping my derriere...once again latched on.

About that time Mama rounded the corner and once again apologized saying, "He just hasn't learned 'personal space' yet."

A million thoughts ran thru my head, the first being, Seriously? then followed by, Get this thing off me and finally, Personal Space? Oh, I find this personal, now give me some space.

Mama then disappeared around the corner and "little one" looked up, head still in my bosoms and said, "You're sexy."

All righty then...I fear Mama may be a taaaaaad misguided on "little one."

I reached around and pried his little fingers loose and removed him from my body saying, "We need to find your mother." I then pulled "little one" like you would a sack of laundry, out the front door to Mama waiting on the porch.

"She looked at him smiling and said, "Oh...are you bothering this nice lady again?"

I gave her his hand and said "Still...he's bothering me still. Oh...and he has quite a vocabulary to be so small."

She looked at me, embarrassed and said, "I'm so sorry, he gets this from watching his dad."

As I locked the door I thought...NOTE TO SELF... Turn down dinner invitation from family...and avoid Dad.

∘ ∘ ◕ ◔ ∘ ∘

James left a cookie on his desk and ran to a closing. It's just sitting there all chocolately and delicious looking...it's like it's calling me. Does this man not know me at all? Oh, the humanity...

I discovered today while showing a house that the most prominent thing I remember from school is Never - Enter - Santa's - Workshop. I believe in 2nd grade I was taught this to remember North - East - South - West. As of now I am still working on the directional part of it...

○ ○ ◐ ● ◑ ○ ○

Sitting here returning emails and thinking back to when I worked at Waterloo. One day I left my email open and one of the guys I worked with changed my signature/closing from "Yours sincerely, Jana" to "For a Good Time Call Jana." Didn't discover it for a few days... Corporate didn't find it humorous but on the bright side my social calendar did fill up...

○ ○ ◐ ● ◑ ○ ○

Wonders if it is possible to hook an electric fence to a Real Estate sign...Just wondering...

○ ○ ◐ ● ◑ ○ ○

Tracked across 120 acres today with a family from Jonesboro...all uphill mind you...rocks and gulley's and tracks the elder gentleman identified as bear...

The last 1/4 mile of the journey the only comfort I could find was when I glanced down and saw my name tag and thought at least that would help them identify me...

A few months ago I met a lovely young couple that was searching for a home. We looked high, we looked low, we laughed, we cried, we ate things...we looked at something like 762 homes before they finally settled on one...that was For Sale By Owner...but all in all...I feel we bonded...fast forward to now...I just received a big ol' bag of every kind of homemade treat you can imagine! This reaffirms my motto...WILL WORK FOR FOOD...

As the Real Estate Agent slammed on her brakes and did the soccer mom arm fling move to the passenger seat, she realized there was no hope for her half eaten cupcake...as the cupcake tumbled to the floor and was covered with files, plat books and a ceramic Elvis, the agent made a promise to herself...and to others...to ALWAYS finish her pastry before getting behind the wheel...God Speed my friends...God speed.

Sitting in a home I just showed waiting on my next showing of it, wishing the home owners wouldn't bake these things that smell soooooo good and are making my mouth water right before they leave...it's a conspiracy I tell you...

Yesterday I showed homes to a couple I aspire to be in twenty years...she is a sassy, spunky woman who refuses to wear her seatbelt and worships her twelve grandchildren and he is an older gentleman who is debonair enough to capture the heart of a woman twenty years his junior and may I add, I find quite charming... They narrowed it down to three...the outside of one, the setting of another and the inside of a third...has anyone seen my magic wand?

Waiting on my people at the home I'm showing at ten and pondering...do I have enough time to eat the chocolate cake the home owners left me and if not will my prospective home buyers expect me to share...

Just introduced myself to a prospective client and he said..."Yeah, I remember you. Didn't you use to hang out down at the County Jail?"
I feel we made a connection...

To the person who put my sign in the tree at Stubblefield Road...I am sorry to inform you that particular Sycamore is sold...

Could I show you something in a Pine?

Left the office yesterday morning at nine-thirty for what was to be a one farm showing. Come two p.m. I am still in the boondocks showing farms. I receive a text from the office...

OFFICE:	Are you ok?
ME:	And if I say "No"?
OFFICE:	We will come find you.
ME:	We need a better alert system...

I don't know if they were actually concerned or just wondering how much longer they had peace and quiet...I suspect the latter...

Termite Company dropped off paperwork for me. James put it on my desk with a Tootsie Roll on top of it...he said so I would be sure and notice it. I don't know which is sadder...his image of me or the fact that it worked...

As I sat at the closing table with the 79-year-old man and his wife, whom I had only met the week before when writing up his offer, the man turned to me and said, "I need to speak to you young lady!"

Feeling as though I had been scolded I said, "Yes, sir?"

He proceeded to tell me that he had been worried to death that I had got in his truck to look at the property after only knowing him for 5 minutes.

I said, "Well sir, there are 3 things you didn't realize,"

1) When you got out to open the gate, I texted my location, your name and type of vehicle to my co-worker and received confirmation that he had my back.

2) I had a pistol in my purse you didn't know about... and last but not least...

3) I think I could have out run you...

He and his wife just grinned and then he replied shaking his head, "Well...I had 2 guns in the truck and I think I could have caught you...unless you started up one of them damn hills...

∘ ∘ ○ ● ○ ∘ ∘

My 1:00 stood me up, didn't call and didn't answer when I called...I'm having high school dating flashbacks... Color me rejected...

Yesterday morning, I was having some trouble with my new do. It was my floor day, so I texted the office and told them I was running late due to "female issues." I received a text back that said, "Not to worry, got it covered, take your time."

It was at this point I realized I could probably skip a week claiming "female issues," and no one would say a word for fear of me explaining what "female issues" were.

All righty then...I see a mini vacation in my future!

⚬ ◦ ◉ ◦ ◦

It is a daily argument in the office between the guys and me as to who will drive. To appointments, to get lunch, to run errands, anywhere...they argue.

Caleb always has too much stuff in his truck and Allen doesn't have gas, so...I drive quite a bit just to shut them up. Seriously...daily argument. Yesterday we were on agent tours and I rode ahead with Stanley. Caleb, Allen and James, the "3-T's," as Stanley calls them, were to meet us after their appointments at one of the homes.

We finished with the home and were wondering where the "3-T's were. As we walked out on the front porch, Stanley said they were probably arguing on who would drive.

Right about that time here they come up the road...in *my* Jeep. The moment was priceless! Well played gentleman...well played.

I have a client from Texas that arrived last night to see 20+ farms in 5 counties this week. I am showing her 5 today and then sending her to meet Cathy Johnson in Ash Flat to look at some, then back here later in the week to see more. She was worried about traveling here alone, because she said she was, "Directionally Challenged."

I feel we will bond well...

On a side note, I drive a 2005 white Jeep Liberty with license plate JANA...just in case we run out of bread crumbs and can't find our way home...

I seem to be having some issues lately with my signs ending up in yards of homes that are not presently for sale and people calling wanting to purchase said home.

I had 5 misplaced yesterday. Kinda like Where's Waldo for Real Estate...so, if you happen to end up with one of my signs in your yard and your home is not for sale, please call the number on top and I will retrieve it.

Or...if you are feeling froggy and you like how the sign looks, I can bring over the paperwork and we can sell that bad boy...

And remember...call Carter Realty for all your Misplaced Signage Needs!

TYPICAL CONVERSATION AT CARTER REALTY...

An older couple walks in and sits at Barry's desk.
ME: (whispering) Who are they?
STANLEY: (whispering) They are Barry's parents. Yeah,
      I think they are Barry's parents.
BARRY: (shaking hands) Hello, I'm Barry Ford. Nice to
      meet you.
STANLEY: (whispering) Ok...they aren't Barry's parents.
JAMES: Maybe he just hasn't seen them in awhile...
ME: Barry's parents seem nice...

◦ ◦ ● ◦ ◦

As the Real Estate agent leaned over the ledge to grab her sign little did she know the forces that be, said..."Hey, watch this..."

And now she sits locked out of her office and out of her vehicle with her keys at the bottom of the drainage ditch...in the rain...good one Murphy...good one."

◦ ◦ ● ◦ ◦

Early for my appointment, so I'm pondering...

I suspect the excitement I feel when I see a For Sale by Owner is somewhat similar to a hunter's excitement when a 10 point buck steps into range...

I was showing an old man some property and we came across what he identified as a really good looking coon hound. He started reminiscing about the good ol' days and said, "You know...coon hunting is just an excuse for men to run around in the woods with flashlights, drink whiskey and shoot guns." Then he asked me if I'd ever been coon hunting.

I said, "No, but I had been "Snipe" hunting a time or two."

He spit out his chew, snickered a little and said, "Same thing...different result..."

I walked onto the deck ahead of my client. She pointed out the landscaping in the back yard. I moved closer to get a good look and glanced down at the flower pot on the rail. Upon a second glance I noticed a snake hanging out of it...

As I tried to fly backwards to no avail, I took out the chair, the client and the dog's water bowl before being stopped by the back door.

My client said "oops" and grabbed the rubber snake out of the pot. "I put that in there to scare off the birds...I guess it works on Real Estate Agents too," she said giggling.

I feel we bonded...

I've been pondering some numbers. I roughly deal with probably 40 clients a day via walk-ins, appointments, email, phone calls, showings, listings, inquiries etc...

You multiply that by 365 days a year, which is around 15,000 clients alone that I interact with in a year, not to mention everyone else I run across. Granted I don't work every day but some days are busier than normal. Statistically, out of those 15,000 people, some of them are gonna be nuts. I seem to have my share hence my stories on FB. Yeah, you know who you are...

Anyway, yesterday I shot the statistics through the roof when another agent and I went to an impromptu showing waaaaaaaaaaaay out in the boonies. Folks, we are talking Banjo Country. I drive to the property, get out and introduce myself and my coworker to 4 seemingly nice adults. The oldest gentleman was having a little trouble walking and it crossed my mind that he might be handicapped. Never did I dream he was drunk as a skunk along with the rest of the family. Luckily the driver, a woman, was not partaking in the drinking.

As the showing unfolded the eldest "gentleman" repeated, "I will write you a check for $59,900," at least a 100 times...it was almost like background music.

The woman was trying to help the man walk while what I assume were the 2 adult sons, split up and staggered in different directions. It was like a daycare trying to wrangle them all in one area to make them leave, once we discovered what the problem was.

The agent with me kept his cool and spouted positive things such as, "We will call the owners and ask them the questions you have," and "Well, let's go back to the office and write that offer up," while the man in the background kept yelling, "I'll write you a check for $59,900."

The agent has grandkids and is more used to dealing with 2-year-olds than I am. We finally got Otis loaded and as we watched them leave the property the agent turned to me and said, "Do you ever have normal showings?"

He is obviously NOT on FB...

As I watched my client retrieve a wet wipe to clean the bird poo off his shirt, the whole "bird-poo-lucky-could-be-your-perfect-home," speech went thru my mind...but I could tell from the amount of wet wipes he had to use, I should just move along...

Gotta pick your moments folks...Gotta pick your moments...

Brenda Bettis got us a motion activated M & M's dispenser for the office. Every time I walk by, it just spits a pile out whether I'm close or not. I don't know whether to be offended or feel special.

Just had lunch with "Man from Florida." He said "I was the Life of the Party…"

"The Stick that Stirred the Drinks"…

I like that…

As we left the garage to make our way to the shop, a squirrel was pointed out as potential breakfast by my client. Across the yard at the gazebo, I spotted what I swore to be deer tracks. While all of us were examining the shop, I found tracks that in my mind were large enough to belong to a bear.

"I found bear tracks over here!" I exclaimed.

This was followed up by "Are you sure they weren't Squatch tracks?" by my client.

Curses…amateur mistake…everyone know Squatch trumps bear. Well played Mr. Sharp…well played.

I'm exhausted. Seriously contemplated napping at my desk this afternoon, but they seem to frown on that. I don't think it was the actual napping that bothered them, but when I kicked off my shoes, pulled a teddy bear out of the drawer and started sucking my thumb, I might have gone too far.

Go figure…

Real Estate Tip #33

When at a property trying to secure a listing, it is probably in your best interest NOT to back over Grandma Pat's prize rose bush...OR Grandma Pat when she is running to stop you...

Met an agent at a referral listing yesterday. The home owner was at work, so we went in to take pictures and do paperwork. I didn't know this agent very well, so I was making small talk about the weather, food and how the Dow closed less than a point away from a new 5 year high...just to pass the time while we waited.

In my attempt to fill the rest of our alone time, I asked her how she knew the home owner.

She said, "Well, it's a long story, but it's my husband's ex-wife."

All righty then...this is getting interesting now...

Approximately 23 minutes into our 40 acre hike, we were all swapping stories about what extremity we were freezing off...

I commented that my ears were pretty much numb...

It was at that point, the elderly gentleman giggled a little and pointed out my unused hood...

I feel it was a bonding moment...

My first "floor day" alone here at Carter Realty and I wrote up 3 listings, delivered an offer on a home and just watered a plastic plant...they may not leave me alone again...

· ○ ◉◉◉ ○ ·

Actual property line description given by agent earlier today...

The line starts there by the NO HUNTING sign and runs right along the trees just behind the outhouse.

The buyer never even batted an eye...

Welcome to Arkansas!

· ○ ◉◉◉ ○ ·

The housing market is hopping, interest rates are at record lows and more people are moving to Arkansas and trading up than ever before.

Whether they are buying their first home, their retirement home or their dream home...there is one question that seems to be a prominent factor in deciding on a purchase...

"Is is private enough I can pee off the porch?"

It's the simple pleasures life has to offer that we cherish most.

I will admit, I'm not "horse people." I think they are beautiful animals and I envy those that can ride, but after a bad experience when I was 5 and a few since, I suspect my fear of horses will never go away.

Yesterday I started across the pasture to show the barn and I made a large circle around the horses standing by the fence. This was apparently noticed by my client.

He questioned me on it and I told him my story and finished off with, "And they bite!"

He laughed and gave me the Encyclopedia Britannica version of horses. During the tutorial part of the exhibit, he approached the horse, showing me how to pet it, showed me its teeth and talked about how gentle and playful they can be.

As my teacher made his way back toward the hind-end for what I was anticipating to be a riveting speech, the gentle giant turned around and bit the begeebies out of the gentleman's arm.

As I glared at my teacher over my sunglasses, he turned to face me and said, "Point taken," and headed for the barn.

I live for moments like this...

Was showing a home to a couple earlier today when we noticed the woman's earring was missing. While backtracking to find it, the client said, "Well, if we don't find it, we could probably get this house A LOT cheaper after the divorce."

Hold on...I might have a new marketing strategy...

• ○ ◉ ○ ○ •

I was showing property yesterday to a large group of family members, some visiting for the holiday, I presume. I could tell right off they weren't interested in the property, so basically, I was just following them around while everyone visited and I was people watching...one of my favorite things, you know...

Out of the corner of my eye, I noticed a small blonde girl following me, maybe 5 or 6 I would guess, although I feel her mind works on a much higher level...

As the little blonde, whom I have nicknamed Adrian, closely approached, I could sense something was up...like I was being stalked. I found myself trying to keep up with the pack, not lag behind...I watch Animal Planet, I know what happens to the last gazelle.

As Adrian caught up with me, I noticed a large switch in one hand and a cookie in the other. My hope was for the cookie, but no...I got the switch right across my bare legs with the mighty thrust equivalent to a major league player swinging a bat.

As stick hit skin, I yelled out like a five-year-old girl and Adrian dropped the stick...

The family turned around, all one hundred twelve of them, looking for a reason for the outburst. At this point, I felt outnumbered and I dropped my head and said, "I stumped my toe," although you would think the dripping blood from my leg would have given it away.

Adrian ran ahead to her mom and the family thanked me for my time and said they would call. I retreated back toward my Jeep like a wounded pup as I watched the little girl skipping off laughing...

Adrian—1...Agent—0...

* ◦ ◦ ● ◦ ◦ •

Went next door to look at the remodel of our new office last night. They had the walls placed for my cubicle so I got to see where I would sit. My desk is strategically placed where I can see the highway, still see everyone else in the room and is exactly the same distance from my desk to the front door, the bathroom and the kitchen.

This architect is a freaking genius!

* ◦ ◦ ● ◦ ◦ •

That awkward moment when you walk your clients around to the backyard to see the beautiful view, just to find that the home owner's dogs really, really like each other. I mean seriously fond of one another...

ME: I need to show your home at 9 a.m. tomorrow,
           please.
CLIENT: Great! Break a leg!
ME: The buyer is a 90-year-old man.
CLIENT: Scratch that last text. Don't break anything,
           okay?
ME: Good plan.
    It helps to have all the facts...

• ○ ◉●◉ ○ •

Yesterday, an older couple came in the office and I realized they were both my teachers from grade school. I just happened to have a *Stars* magazine with me on the cover on my desk, so I took them one, introduced myself and asked if they remembered me.

The gentleman looked at the magazine, looked back at me and said, "Jana Brown...Jana Brown...didn't you talk a lot?"

Ahhhh...he DOES remember me!

Back from my five farm excursion. Topics covered today:

"Why are there hogs on everyone's vehicle?"

"My husband said I had to find a place he could walk around naked on, not that we do that," and last, but not least...

"I really can't wait to move up here and be able to gain weight like you."

I feel we bonded...

I showed a home to a couple in Little Rock today. He is from here, but she grew up in the city. The home is 10.7 miles down a gravel road. She seemed a bit frustrated with the lack of cell phone signal, the seven flooded creeks we drove through and the numerous hills, curves, and potholes in 10 miles of gravel.

I was doing my best to convince her this is not that much different than the city, just more gravel and more peace and quiet, when we topped the hill to meet a donkey drawn cart with a man driving, who had a shotgun across his lap and a pig...yes a pig...following close behind...

It was at that point I feel I lost her...

I was helping show a home with another agent who was not familiar with the property. I followed him and his 50-something-year-old client into the kitchen. I pointed out how the appliances looked brand new and that they had the owner's manuals taped to them.

The agent said, "You know, when I was in high school, all the time, my mother used to try to fix me up with these girls from church and she always said, "But son, they are pretty in the face."

The client nodded in agreement and moved on to the living room.

ME: Blank stare...The home remains unsold, but I feel the agent and his client bonded on a level above anything I have ever achieved. I remain in awe...

◦ ◦ ● ● ● ◦ ◦ ·

Yesterday, I got a call from a man in Ohio on some property on Eleven Point River. He asked about snakes. Said his wife had seen a show about cowboys crossing a river and there was a bunch of snakes.

I said, "You were watching *Lonesome Dove.* Twenty minutes later, we had discussed, *Lonesome Dove, North and South* Part I because we both hated Part II without Swayze, antique furniture, his wife going through menopause, hot flashes, shipping costs, deer hunting, peach pie and back to the property...which he made a verbal offer on.

We didn't cover pickup trucks, Mama or trains, but I feel we hit the high points...

• • • ● ● • •

Everyone in the office is always bringing leftovers, a new recipe they are trying out, or even just goodies for each other—just because.

A friend of mine was making "Cake in a Jar" around Valentine's Day, so I got them for everyone in the office. Bright pinks, blues and green frosting on delicious baked cakes! YUMMY!

A few days later, I was asking if they had tried them. One agent said, "I ate the entire thing, my wife didn't get any of it."

Another one said, "Oh, I loved it! Made my poo pink. I've never had pink poo. I tried to get my wife to come look at it, but she wouldn't. I have pictures though...

I have yet to hear from the one that got the neon green frosting, but I suspect we will have photos to post there also...

Sometimes the comfort level in the office is overwhelming...

Sometimes it takes awhile for clients to find their dream home and it is a very exciting journey for all involved. It is an important step in life and I feel blessed that they include me.

I have one client who had a little baby when we started looking for homes. That little baby is now a sweet, shiny, intelligent two-year-old girl.

Saturday, we were looking a home and I was carrying her. I was pointing at pictures on the wall, asking what it was. One by one, she said what was in the painting...horse, turkey, cow, train...

As we made our way back to the living room, she pointed to a beautiful statue on the mantle and said, "Catholic."

OMG! This child is brilliant! I was so impressed and overwhelmed, I was telling everyone, "She said Catholic... she is a baby genius!"

I decided to test her even farther and pointed to a clock on the wall with a picture of a beautiful peacock on it.

She looked at me and said, "Clock?"

Okay...well, I should have seen that one coming, but OMG...she said Catholic!

Stanley had an appointment, but was expecting a semi-truck load of carpet squares to be delivered for the new office and asked James to watch for it.

I, manning the phones, stayed behind while the "men folk" made their way to the construction site. James, Allen and Bill, in single file, marched to the back of the truck. I refrained humming *The Three Stooges* theme song for fear of retaliation.

James, being the "planner" he is, had a five page outline on how it should be done, complete with graphs and a pie chart. He grabbed one box and hit the door.

Allen, who owned a carpet business for years, was stating how he had been unloading carpet longer than the two of them had been alive and grabbed two boxes and headed for the door.

The "peeing contest" continued as three and then four boxes were carried from the truck to the office area.

Bill, the smart one, in my opinion, was still on his first box. I'm not sure how the contest ended, but Bill got in his truck and went home. Allen and James bumped chests and limped back to the office and I can't get the stench of testosterone out of the air.

I feel my positive feminine influence is dying a little more every day...

I walked out of the building after a long, long, long day and was startled by a man across the parking lot making smooching noises, whistling and clapping his hands at me. After the day I had, I was in no mood for this.

I took off my sunglasses, put my hands on my hips, cocked my head sideways for maximum effect and said, "You have got to be kidding me! Does that ever work for you?" I then followed it up with "Moron."

It was at this point a little dog ran out from under the car beside me and jumped right into the man's arms.

Well, lookey there...it does work. I'll be hiding in my room is anyone needs me...

• ∘ ◉ ◉ ∘ •

A few years back, I was sitting in my office doing paperwork. It was early August and well over a hundred degrees outside. A tall, well-dresed man in a suit came in and approached my desk. He told me that his van had broken down, pointing to a black minivan on the side of the street out front, and asked if he could wait in the office until his back-up got there. Told him, "Of course!" and the gentleman took a seat on the sofa. He seemed a bit fidigty and once again approached my desk.

MAN: Let me tell you what's about to happen.

ME: Ooookkkkaaayyy. What's about to happen? (Having flashback to Forensic Files and quietly searching for my letter opener).

MAN: Well, there's a body in my van and I didn't want to scare you.

ME: Oh, you're scaring me.

MAN: I work for a funeral home and I just picked up a body.

ME: I would have led with that.

MAN: When the other van shows up, we're going to move the body from my van to the other and I wanted you to be prepared.

ME: Well, it's in a coffin, right?

MAN: No, it's on a stretcher.

ME: Well, you covered it with a sheet or something, didn't you?

MAN: No, it's too hot outside.

ME: Blank stare

MAN: I'll just wait on the porch outside.

ME: Sounds good.

We didn't have coffee or snacks, but I feel we bonded...

We were at a company function when an elderly gentleman walks up to one of our agents, sticks out his hand to shake and said, "Colonel Winston Bryant. I was with the First Provisional Marine Brigade and arrived at Pusan, South Korea, August 2, 1950. You are an Army man, aren't you?"

The agent shook the man's hand and the two launched into a long conversation about military life, the State of the Union, surface-to-air missiles and the reasons behind the Vietnam War. It was like watching reruns of *Baa Baa Black Sheep*.

When the gentleman disappeared back into the crowd, I turned to the agent, very impressed with the conversation, and stated, "I didn't know you were in the Army."

He said, "Oh, I wasn't. I just couldn't bring myself to break the old guys heart."

Well done my friend, well done...

As I was driving my client from one home to another yesterday evening, we were enjoying the nice scenery while the four-year-old in her car seat was pointing out the animals along the way. We passed several cows and goats with the little girl making farmyard sounds from the back seat.

Her Nana was in the front with me telling her, "Look at this sweetie, how does a goat go?" and "What does a cow say?"

We rounded the corner to find a huge amount of what I learned to be Doves in the road.

About the time Nana got, "Oh, honey, look at the beautiful Doves," out...it was too late.

The feathers were flying and I had a new hood ornament.

Nana turned to me, eyes widened in disbelief and all I could think was "Coo coo."

It's been a good career thus far...I'll miss it.

Spousal Unit

ME: We are going to the movie this weekend.

SPOUSAL UNIT: I'd rather eat dirt.

ME: Well pack some then. It has been three years. You Are taking me to a movie. Adapt. What do you want to see?

SPOUSAL UNIT: Fine...Wild Hogs 2 or that one where the Corvette is chasing the Camaro thru the corn field.

ME: I guess I can Google Corvette chasing Camaro in corn field and see what comes up but I don't think Wild Hogs 2 is out.

SPOUSAL UNIT: Okay, we can just wait till it comes out to go then.

ME: No, I don't think it's even been made yet. I don't think they're making one. We can't go see Wild Hogs 2!

SPOUSAL UNIT: Why do you refuse to cooperate?

∙ ∘ ◦ ● ◦ ∘ ∙

I lit a candle, blew out the match and handed it to Mike to throw away. He thought I handed him a toothpick with something chocolate on it. We really need to invest in some stronger glasses...

Mike and I were discussing the "What Ifs" last night...
Such as...What if...I really could publish a book, What
if...we won the lottery and What if...Tassimo lowered the
cost of its coffee. All of which seem to be out of reach
dreams.

He looked at me, gave me that knowing glare and
said, "If you can give away a pregnant cat, you can sell a
book."

While I do appreciate my husband's efforts to boost
my ego and his faith in my ability in sales, does anyone
else find it odd that our "Life's Goals" are measured
against giving away a knocked up feline?

• ○ ◐ ● ◑ ○ •

The Spousal Unit went to "work" in the barn for a
couple hours last night and it occurred to me I haven't
been in the barn in close to three years.

I attempted to visit him unannounced one day and
was greeted by two snakes approximately twenty feet
long—each. Pythons, I believe.

He stated those were his "good snakes" that kill the
"bad snakes." Like there is a difference?

Anyway, it also occurred to me he could be keeping
another family down there and I wouldn't know.
Hmmm...Glad I got the good house.

My hubby got me an hour massage. Never had one. The office is right next door to my tax lady's office...I feel he really thought this gift through...

Ten years ago tonight when Mike was still a date and not my dear sweet husband...he took me to Lazzari's in Jonesboro for a candlelight dinner. It was to be an eventful night and I had NO idea it was coming!!

We had our supper, drove back to Pocahontas, stopped at a friend's house for a short visit and drove on out to my little cabin on the river and what came next was not expected...yes, you guessed it...HE DUMPED ME! He came back in February and we were married the next October but yep...dumped me...ended it...kicked me to the curb...Hasta la vista, baby...We reminisce every year about this time...

Mike gave me ice cream to tide me over while he makes me potato soup. Reminds me of the Ron White skit where he says, "That will shut her up...for a minute."

As I lay in bed, begging for sleep, I tried to block the "outside" noises to no avail. I need silence when trying to sleep and there seemed to be some extra little distractions I'm not used to. First I could hear the kids in the other room, then there was the TICK...TICK...TICK...of Mike's clock he just received as a gift and, to add to the madness there was the mini electric heater, that for some reason he had decided needed to be in the bathroom...kicking on and kicking off...kicking on and kicking off...kicking on and kicking off...

The Spousal Unit noticed me tossing and turning... because I meant for him to...and finally asked what the problem was.

After telling him my list of sleep killers, he kindly got up, unplugged the heater, closed the bedroom door, took the battery out of the clock and then lay back down.

"Now," he said, "you are taken care of, but I seem to have one more annoying thing on my list and after ten years of marriage, I have yet to find the switch to turn it off."

I'm not for sure, but I think it is very possible he was aiming that remark at me...very possible...

Mike just turned The Muppets 12 Days of Christmas up on the radio. I don't know whether to hug him or make fun of him...

Mike cooked about a five-hundred pound ham all night for the festivities this afternoon. Smelling it all night sure affected/effected that whole "Visions of Sugarplums Danced in their Head" line. Mine leaned towards dancing pigs...

Mike has to go into Bed, Bath & Beyond today to pick up one item. I'll admit it, he's scared. He has heard stories and has seen photos of the madness, although never experienced it firsthand.

I'm trying to make it into a sporting event to lessen the blow, kinda like deer hunting on a refuge or maybe fishing in a tournament with several boats. I fear it is not working.

I swear I heard him saying "One please" in his sleep. There was even night sweats and pacing. It's not pretty folks. Please keep him in your thoughts and prayers today. God speed my dear man...God speed...

Mike just brought me a forgotten box of White Chocolate Covered Oreos...I bet this is what winning the Pulitzer is like...

Mike and I went out to a "fancy" restaurant Monday night. He was looking at the various salads or "Cold beginnings" as they labeled it and finally settled on a traditional Caesar salad because he said that was the only one he recognized.

When they brought our "cold beginning" Mike looked down, then looked at me and whispered, "Who the heck put a raw fish on my salad?"

Seriously...there was a nice pretty green salad with what appeared to be a small perch or what I always called "bait" right smack dab on top.

I told him Caesar salad dressing has anchovies in it, aka fish. He then stated he thought he ordered a salad with artichokes not anchovies...How redneck are we?

· ○ ◉●◐ ◑ ○ ·

Kitchen table...coat rack...kitchen table...coat rack... apparently these two things mean the same when speaking male...

· ○ ◉●◐ ◑ ○ ·

Sometimes Mike will throw a load of clothes in the washer when I'm gone, or he has just gutted a deer or he is guilty of something. Yesterday I put a "fragile" shirt in the dirty clothes basket and told him just in case he washed some, not to wash it. He said not to worry; he NEVER washed anything soft or shiny...

There was a milestone decision made at Caldwell Manor last night...the whip cream will be stored in the door of the fridge, not on the top shelf.

You see it's apparently too hard to move the whip cream canister two inches to the side to get to the Spousal Units iced tea pitcher...I am really at peace with this decision and I know I FINALLY rested last night for the first time in weeks...It's times like this...when we work together...that makes this marriage run like a fine-oiled machine...

MARITAL TIP #23...While half asleep and making your way to the kitchen for a drink at 2 a.m...Do not wake your spouse with a blood curdling scream UNTIL you are sure there is a stranger in the living room and not the lamp you moved earlier that day...

I yawned like forty-five minutes ago and while doing so hit some button on the remote that has left me with a blank screen.

Mike is home now trying to diagnose the problem. He is leaning towards that problem being me. I am currently banned from all electronics...

While I was getting ready to go out Saturday night I put on a dress and heels and asked Mike how I looked.

"You aren't wearing that dress, are you?" was his response.

Apparently it resembled a tablecloth his grandma owned. So I put on jeans and a shirt and came back in to get his opinion...

"Well...it's better than the dress." I did not seek his approval on my third and final choice...

⋅ ∘ ● ◉ ● ∘ ⋅

I have a slight memory of my spaceship coffee maker accidently going off at midnight, Mike saying, "I hear a 4 wheeler" and the front door closing. Now there is mud in the floor, seventy-three blackbirds in the front yard and the faint smell of coconut in the air...Holy cow, how sound do I sleep?"

⋅ ∘ ● ◉ ● ∘ ⋅

Sitting with my husband...I was texting a client, on the phone with another and had another calling... answered him, made some notes and continued texting.

I glanced at Mike who was staring and said, "My life is crazy!"

He went back to reading and said, "My wife is crazy."

Getting kinda cold to sleep in the yard, don't you think?

Mike said he will be glad when I'm done with my "50 Shades" books...says he misses the background noise of me jabbering...

His romantic words melt my heart...

MIKE: We are having a health fair and Steve Shultz is one of the speakers.

ME: What is he going to speak on? How to fry up a healthy rooster? Oh, I know, how to sleep better with loud noises outside.

MIKE: How to deal with unruly neighbors.

ME: Or that...

Trying to make manly small talk with Mike...

ME: I saw at least ten deer together yesterday while showing property. Why were so many in a group like that?

MIKE: They like each other.

ME: That's your scientific explanation?

MIKE: They aren't kin.

I feel it was a bonding moment for us both...

4:01 a.m. — footsteps on porch

4:02 a.m. — Mike arises and goes to LR window to investigate with two guard cats following

4:05 a.m. — They return to BR and look out window

4:06 a.m. — LR then BR, LR then BR, LR then BR

4:10 a.m. — He suspects it is a possum

4:11 a.m. — LR then BR, LR then BR...

4:12 a.m. — ME: "Is there a person on the porch?"
MIKE: "No."

4:13 a.m. — ME: "Then lay down your gun and come back to bed."
MIKE: "Okay."

4:14 a.m. — Mike goes to little boys room...

4:15 a.m. — MIKE: "There's a critter in the back yard, I think it's a fox."

4:15 a.m. — back to window...

Lesson learned...Fox trumps possum...and apparently wife too...

I walked in last night to Mike making supper, he turned and said, "I put..."

I stopped him short with the "talk to the hand" move and said, "Please Baby, Just let me get my boots off and I will be right back."

He nodded and went back to cooking and I opened the door to the bedroom to change clothes. About two minutes into my disrobing, he came to the door and said, "What I was going to tell you was that I set my game camera up on the dresser, testing to see if it worked. I needed a dark room."

Well now...isn't that special...LESSONS LEARNED HERE...1)Listen to your husband...2)That saying, "dance like no one is watching"...not so much...3) Modeling is definitely not my forte...That's all I've got to say about that...

CAKE PLATE UPDATE: While retrieving a dishtowel, The Spousal Unit pulled the bottom drawer out, which in turn hit the cake plate, which in turn somehow wedged his toe between the cake plate and the floor. I have to be honest. It wasn't pretty. There were words. Ohhhhh, the words...for a moment I thought the new storage place for the cake plate would be as far as he could throw it from the back deck. But alas he recovered and it is safe and sound back in the kitchen floor. I have only one word for this...WINNING!

Yesterday was a very long and action packed day with Mom going into the Home in Walnut Ridge for a sabbatical, then to the office for real estate, squeezing in some Ducks Unlimited donation stuff and then running home to get ready for the funeral home. Mike was going up later than I, so I laid out the clothes for him to wear. We left the funeral home around eight, grabbed a quick bite and headed home. I'm sitting on the bed covered in paperwork, fighting off Demon Cat, bandaging my feet, charging my phone while texting a client and trying to make sense of a contract...

Mike comes to the door taking off his yellow shirt that I had laid out for him and asks me, "Is my yellow shirt dirty?"

Sometimes I feel I coddle him too much...

• ○ ●◐● ○ •

The Spousal Unit is contemplating a zip line from the house to his deer stand...that way there is no scent from walking...I've seen this look in his eye before...it usually ends with a trip to the Emergency Room. Hold me...

Every year it seems putting the tree together is the least wanted task in the Caldwell household. Love decorating it, but I can never get the branches in the correct slots and it hurts my little delicate hands.

Mike was hunting so Steph and I decided to bestow the privilege upon Kyle, the newbie. Sweet little guy took it as an "I'm really part of the family now" gesture and dove in head first.

Steph and I stared in awe of how meticulous he was at fluffing and arranging every branch.

Mike gets back, walks in and said, "Did we get a new tree? It never looked that good before. Oh...you suckered the new guy into doing it."

I am halfway ashamed that I never put forth the effort to poof our tree before to its maximum beauty and halfway wondering who we will get to do it next year since Mike has blown our cover...Traitor...

· ∘ ◦ ◉ ◦ ∘ ·

There was a new *Chopped* on TV last night and I yelled at Mike so he wouldn't miss it. I said, "Ohhh, it's a cool one! It's people like you cooking." (Meaning not professional chefs).

He said, "You mean people whose wives don't cook?"

Standing on the deck looking across the river...

    MIKE: Look, There is something over there.
    ME: Is it a Sasquatch?
    MIKE: It's a coyote. No, it's too healthy to be a coyote.
    ME: It's a Squatch.
    MIKE: Surely it's not a wolf?
    ME: S-Q-U-A-T-C-H!!!
    MIKE: It must be someone's German Shepherd.

At times I feel I'm ignored...

                ∘ ∘ ◉ ◯ ∘ ∘ ∘

The conversation in my bed after a 3:30 a.m. text...

    MIKE: David Statler?
    ME: YEP.
    MIKE: He kill something?
    ME: Nope, he wants pie.
    MIKE: Pie? Now?
    ME: No, he wanted it this afternoon.
    MIKE: Why didn't you give it to him? We'd be asleep
           right now.
    ME: I know...
    BTW: Your pie is in the oven as we speak...

Came home to find "hoodlums" running amuck on our property. Mike chased them and they ran into the woods. I don't think they realize he sees a moving target as a challenge...

Took a short nap and dreamed I was making fishing lures. Seriously? For the love of Bill Dance...what has this man done to me?

I believe marriage is about choices and compromise...I gave Mike the choice of watching *Cupcake Wars* or *The Oscars*...as a compromise, he went to the barn...working together is what it's all about...

I received the phone call no wife ever wants to get...Mike called about 5:30 from home to tell me...our air conditioner is not working...this cannot end well for anyone involved...mark my words...

Sometimes I stress out...A few things that stress me are public speaking...hence the hives, I stress over property that hasn't sold when it really needs to and I stress over getting my house straight before company arrives...and it seems the larger the group coming, the more neurotic I am.

Yesterday I was trying to turn "Mike's hunting table" back into our dining room table. He, bless his heart, was "resting" in his recliner because he had got up at 5 a.m. to put the turkey in the oven. Once again, bless his heart.

I took his game camera deer pic viewing thing and moved it to another table out of the way.

He said "I don't really like that there."

I turned, smiled and politely told him, "Well, you could help me, you know..."

"He said, "I did, I told you I didn't like it there."

On a side note...if anyone is looking to purchase one of those game camera deer pic viewing things...just be aware they don't bounce well when thrown.

· · ○ ○●◉●○ ○ ·

The Spousal Unit's AARP Card arrived this week. I placed it unopened on the counter. That was Plan "A."

He didn't open it. Then in Plan "B" I opened it and just left the card on the counter.

Still on the counter. Today I launch Plan "C." I will place it in his wallet and when he opens it, surprise!! I hope Plan "D" doesn't include me sleeping on the couch...

Yay...The Spousal Unit finally fixed my dryer last night. It has been out a week due to hunting season and various other reasons he thought of to avoid tearing it apart.

I had gone thru most of my clean jeans...my two pair of what I call my good jeans first, followed by my jeans that are too long, then my comfy jeans, my yard sale jeans and out of desperation had to wear the ones Mike refers to as "plumbers jeans."

It's been a colorful week...Welcome back Ken, I've missed you!

* * * * * * *

TO THE PEOPLE LOOKING FOR THEIR DOG IN MY YARD LAST NIGHT:

I am really sorry and truly hope you found your puppy. They are precious indeed. I also would like to apologize for what you saw on the porch while looking for said dog.

Who knew when I said to The Spousal Unit, "There is someone outside, I saw lights," it was code for..."Go outside in your underwear, armed, and scare the beejeebus out of those poor people."

Once again please accept my deepest sympathy and maybe next time just call ahead and I will run outside and look for you...

Woke up at 5:15 and tried to strike up a casual conversation with The Spousal Unit. He wasn't too chatty but did ask me to make him some chocolate rolls for breakfast. He never asks for my cooking so I was thrilled! I hopped out of bed, made coffee, gave the kittys their snack and then it hit me...he doesn't eat chocolate rolls for breakfast...he just wanted me out of there so he could sleep! He manipulated me. He diverted my attention like you do a two-year-old. He USED me...Well played Mr. Caldwell...well played...

· ◦ ◉ ◯ ◦ ·

The Spousal Unit came home after being in a school in Little Rock since Wednesday. I was inside and saw him pull up but he didn't come in right away. I waited patiently...the whole time knowing where he was.

As he walked thru the door I could see it in his eyes...he had been to see "her." I had come to grips with the fact that I was in the top three favorites of his life, but I now fear I have been bumped down the list to number four. It's lawnmower, fishing, hunting and then Jana running a sad fourth...Hold me...

Mike was reading his lawnmower manual and said, "Cool, this has an hour meter screen. It tells me if it needs serviced, if it's low on something or if it needs attention of any kind." Then he said, "If only women came with an hour meter..."

I said "This one does, but it's more of an Audio Alert System."

⚬ ⚬ ◖●◗ ⚬ ⚬

Mike just called to tell me that Publisher's Clearinghouse called him to deliver a prize of $950,000. The guys at the office were impressed he called to tell me about the prize and not to ask for a divorce. They all have such high hopes for my future...

⚬ ⚬ ◖●◗ ⚬ ⚬

We have determined the depth of my love for Mike...I'm watching Turtle Man with him...

Over the weekend I went to Bass Pro with The Spousal Unit against my better judgment. While he hung out salivating over boats and jigs, I wandered around in the women's clothing. I actually found some shorts I liked and tried on a pair. Perfect! Loved them so much decided I would get them in two colors, so I grabbed the same size in a different color without trying them on....or so I thought. Went to put them on yesterday and they were too small. Looked at label and they were the same size as the first pair. Baffled by this I asked for assistance from the man in the house. He read the size and it was clearly the wrong size. Handed me his glasses and low and behold, he was correct...I now find myself in a quandary...should I be upset that my rear is too large for the smaller shorts or that I was too blind to get the correct size? Hold me...

Mike is putting together my shoe organizer with *The Bachelor* on TV in the background. He is drinking a glass of wine and repeating after the girls saying, "He made me feel so speeeeecccccial, we just have that connection." and "I'm already falling in looooove."

Surely he can see I'm still in the room...

Last night around two a.m., Turner aka Demon Cat, was scratching on the window...over and over and over...I assumed there was something on the porch, but I don't check those noises out anymore. So...after elbowing the Spousal Unit...over and over and over...he finally awoke to hear the noise also.

He stretched, growled and mumbled something under his breath which I can only assume was "Yes, Dear" and left the bedroom.

I guess he must have stopped to watch deer on his way because I dozed off again. Next thing I know I woke up to hear him say, "There's a KID on the porch again."

I sat straight up in bed and said "Again?"

He said, "Yeah, can I just shoot it or Demon Cat so we can get some sleep?"

After having what I suspect to be a mini stroke and very possibly wetting myself, I regained my senses enough to realize he must have said CAT...puts a whole new spin on the porch situation...

About five-thirty a.m. Mike accused me of waking him up just because I'm awake and bored...said that I poke him in the ribs and then pretend I am still asleep... Well...obviously my technique works, I just need to improve on the execution...

I was watching a show last night and it had a mansion that had thirteen bedrooms and twenty-seven bathrooms. I wondered why twice as many baths?

Mike said, "The guy was really old and maybe he needed them close because he couldn't make it to them as quickly as needed."

Sadly this makes perfect sense to me...

⚬ ◦ ◉ ● ◉ ◦ ⚬

I was melting chocolate in a double boiler I had fashioned last night. I asked Mike to watch it while I went to the little girl's room.

I came back to two more pans on the stove, one with our veggie steamer turned upside down in boiling water and my chocolate on it, the other was just a "test-run" he said...

He had switched stirring spoons and potholders and for some unknown reason had the cornstarch out eyeing it...Good Lord, how long was I gone...

Why must men "hot-rod" everything up?

Pulled over on my way back from Missouri...

POLICE:	License and papers please.
ME:	Yes sir.
POLICE:	Where are you headed?
ME:	Home...well not home, but work...but home as in Pocahontas, Arkansas...to my office. I'm working.
POLICE:	Do you have any weapons or illegal drugs to disclose.
ME:	Yes sir. I mean I don't have drugs. I don't do drugs...I mean...I have a gun...in my seat...a pistol.
LADY IN BOX	Turn around when possible.
POLICE:	Why do you have a weapon, Ms. Caldwell?
ME:	Because my husband is a fanatic about guns. I mean...not in a bad way. I mean, he's a really good man. He just believes in carrying guns and I was traveling so...
POLICE:	Are you prepared to use this weapon Ms. Caldwell?
LADY IN BOX	Turn around when possible...
ME:	I don't understand...you mean...on you? Ummm... well, I don't...you mean...I mean...well it's loaded...is that what you mean? You want to see it?
POLICE:	No ma'am, please don't reach for the firearm.
ME:	Okay...
LADY IN BOX	Recalculating...
POLICE:	Okay, Ms. Caldwell...just slow down...and unload your weapon when I leave.
ME:	Yes, sir...I will...thank you, Sir...

I'm not positive but I'm pretty sure that "Gun Fanatic" remark got Mike on a list somewhere...

Yesterday Mike and I were driving in Missouri. He was looking in his rear view mirror and said, "We are about to get pulled over."

I once again went into concealed gun carry panic mode...I checked my seatbelt (which I always wear), smelled my breath against my hand (even though it was nine a.m. and I wasn't drinking), straightened up the interior of the Jeep (no, I don't know why) and watched the blue lights get closer, trying not to wet myself.

I started apologizing for getting him on that list and told him I'd wait on him while he was in prison...

Right about the time Mike pulled onto the shoulder the State Trooper whizzed by us obviously headed elsewhere.

As I sat there shivering, trying to recover from my near death experience, Mike says, "Dangit...I wanted to show him my gun."

I really hope the orange jumpsuit goes with his pretty blue eyes...

· ◦ ◉ ◯ ◦ ◦ ·

As I made my way to the facilities at two a.m...more than half asleep...I didn't realize The Spousal Unit had left the seat up...I discovered that detail just a few seconds later upon splash down...I suspect this is retaliation for the "gun fanatic" remark...and I fear there is more to come...MUST...STAY...STRONG...

Lying in bed last night...

MIKE: Set your alarm?
ME: Yep...
MIKE: Make your coffee?
ME: Yep...
MIKE: Take your heartburn medicine?
ME: Yep...

Pillow talk sure takes on a whole different meaning in your 40's...

• ∘ ◑ ● ◑ ∘ •

Mike was cleaning out his dresser last night and came into the living room with a "Coupon Book of Favors" I had made him probably ten years ago. He handed me one.

I said, "Wait a minute, how many times have you used this same coupon?"

He replied, "Apparently not enough times for the ink on 'Some restrictions apply' to fade off..."

• ∘ ◑ ● ◑ ∘ •

My husband just woke me up to tell me about a gun...he obviously forgot I know where one is...

You know when you dream you are falling and jerk when you wake up? Well, I did that and when I jerked, I kicked the cat across the bed...

When I leaned over to pet her, I then put my knee in a bad spot...

I asked Mike why he didn't say anything. Well apparently my knee was on the nerve that leads to the vocal cords making it impossible to speak...who knew?

* ∘ ◦ ● ◦ ∘ ⋅

Flipping thru channels I made a deal with Mike. I'd watch *Cops* with him from six to seven if he would watch *Cupcake Wars* with me from seven to eight...

You should have seen the disappointment in his eyes when he discovered *Cupcake Wars* is not women wrestling...

* ∘ ◦ ● ◦ ∘ ⋅

The guy on the Weather Channel said if you hear a low rumbling sound to get under cover...he obviously has never slept next to Mike after cabbage and bean Friday... under cover is the last place you want to go...

ME: Get up...I'm hungry!
MIKE: What do you want?
ME: Something different.
MIKE: You want something different?
ME: Yep!
MIKE: You cooking would be different...

Okay...I gotta give him points for that one...

In his 49 years, my husband has mastered many skills...he can rebuild a small block Chevy in twenty minutes flat, he can shoot Lincoln's eye on a penny at two hundred yards blindfolded and he can fry a mighty mean chicken, yet this brilliant specimen of a man has still not figured out what the heck a spoon rest is for...

To the person who told me to "just punch him in the ribs and pretend to be asleep," to stop Mike's snoring...
Was there a plan "B" and does it come with Band-Aid?

I couldn't decide between Oreos or Nutter Butter's so I bought both.

Mike picked up the open package of Nutter Butters and said, "You must have had a stressful day, you didn't even make it out of the store before eating them."

I'm appalled! Does he think I have NO willpower? Geeze...I didn't open them until I got in the car...

· ∘ ● ◑ ● ∘ ·

While getting ready to go out last night, I realized how things have changed over the years. Even getting ready for a party...I still hadn't figured out what I was going to wear at five p.m. and had to be there at six p.m.

I said, "Let me just try on this one dress for you."

His response, "Oh Lord, this never ends well."

Then we are in the bathroom primping and I catch a glimpse of Mike just right to see about a two foot long hair growing from his ear. I point it out and it was like he had discovered gold...

"Wow! That was a long one! That had to be growing for months. Was that on my ear?" He sounded so proud.

This statement was followed by me saying, "Just shave your ears." Then as I switch to my little black purse I pack all the essentials for a hot night out on the town... lipstick, driver's license, Rolaids, glasses, directions home...

Last night I was trying on dresses for a couple of parties I'm attending. I have no idea why, but I was asking Mike's opinion. He is about as useful in that department as a stump. When asked how it looked, I was getting comments like "okay" and "Isn't that the same one you had on?" Seriously, useless.

I was headed out of the bedroom with my last attempt to fish for a compliment, when Mike slammed the door and said, "Don't come in here!"

I'm thinking okay...this dress is a NO! when he came to the door, opened it and said, "It was the part of the Green Mile where the guard kills Mr. Jingles. I know you hate that part."

Say it with me girls...Awwwww...he may not be the best fashion advisor but he certainly makes up for it in other ways...

Sitting in the car waiting on my five-thirty appointment...catching up on phone calls and, I'm not for certain, but I think I just ended my call to the appraiser with "Love you, bye."

Now I'm wondering what Mike thinks since I ended my call to him with, "I'll meet you at the house in the morning."

I sometimes hear noises in the house, on the porch, outside, etc. and send Mike to investigate. I have come to distinguish how severe the situation is by the steps he takes to prepare before he goes to explore...

Preparation includes, but is not limited to:

1) Turn down TV
2) Turn down TV and turn on light
3) Turn down TV, turn on light and take gun
4) Turn down TV, turn on light, take gun and put on pants
5) Turn down TV, turn on light, take gun, put on pants and hand me a gun

We have yet to launch into *Defcon 5*, but I have peace of mind knowing it is an option...

· ɔ ◉● ɔ · ·

Mike just went outside to listen for turkeys. I'm lying here pondering...if I gobble will he come back to bed...

· ɔ ◉● ɔ ·

Slept with the windows open last night. About 3 a.m., I was awakened by this "blowing" sound outside the window, sat straight up in bed.

The Spousal Unit says, "Shhh, its deer...don't scare them.

I'm thinking...seriously...don't scare them? If I could imitate this "snorting" sound, I could rule the world...

Sometimes...after being married for many years, people get lazy and seem to take the time they have with their spouses for granted.

Mike and I are both crazy busy and it is hard to have that scheduled "date night" that I hear some couples have. We try our best to work through all that and have our special time together, no matter what arises. One thing we do—working towards that goal—happens every Sunday night.

We have our supper, which he cooks, then I do the dishes while he prepares for "date night." First off, we argue over what to watch. I lean towards a show about cupcakes and sprinkles and he leans towards a show about rattlesnakes. We compromise and watch a show about the beautiful journey to find something you have always dreamed of...Squatches.

Mike then clears the bar off while I retrieve a towel to cushion the hard surface. He goes to the drawer in the kitchen and gets all the "tools" a couple needs for a night together and spreads them out on the towel...six bottles of medicine, a pill cutter and two long plastic containers marked Sun-Sat.

Then together we discuss our aches and pains and if that med is working for me and his most recent bout with heartburn...this my friends is sharing...be jealous...be very jealous...

As I lay awake at 3:33 a.m., too tired to get up, but too awake to sleep, I tried the classic sleep techniques to no avail...

I must have tossed and turned enough to wake the Spousal Unit, who leapt, yes he leapt, from the bed straight to the window as if his manly instinct sensed there was a wild animal in the yard. As he stood glaring out the blinds studying every inch of the yard, I found the new entertainment in my sleepless night quite amusing.

"What'cha looking at?" I asked.

"A deer," he responded.

"And where is this deer pray tell?" I playfully asked, just excited to have someone to talk to.

He said, "Same place it was last night."

Tiring quickly of the deer conversation, I said, "Could you be more specific? I missed his location in the nightly Deer Spotting Newsletter."

I have now banned him from his late night deer spotting expedition...

· ○ ●◉◐ ○ ๑ · · · ·

MIKE: Should I heat the blade or just alcohol it?

ME: I'm pretty sure when doing surgery with a pocket knife, the sterilization process is not really an issue...

The Spousal Unit had a nightmare last night. His talking and thrashing around woke me from a sound sleep. He has awakened me from several bad dreams over the years and now I could be there for him. As I watched him sleep and punch at the imaginary objects...maybe too long...I wondered what fear causes his nightmares. Was it spiders...snakes...fear of failure...intruders...what scary thing invades this wonderful, strong man's dreams?

I leaned over him, stroked his hair and said, "Baby, wake up, you're having a bad dream."

His eyes opened and he calmed. Obviously relieved to be released from his dreamland turmoil.

I snuggled up to him, hoping to turn this frightening moment into a tender bonding experience and asked, "What were you dreaming about, Baby?"

He scratched his head, rubbed his eyes and whispered, "Paneling."

We lead such different lives.

· ﹒ ﹒ ● ﹒ ﹒ ·

Lying here in the dark listening to the Spousal Unit talk in his sleep. He said deer and rack...I sure hope he's having a hunting dream...

We have a hunting ritual at Caldwell Manor: Alarm goes off at four a.m., Mike hits the snooze at least three times, finally gets up and stumbles to the window to look for deer...just in case they are outside waiting to be shot, I guess. Closes the door so gently as to not wake me and heads to the coffee pot. The rest is just what I have pieced together from sounds and grunts, but from what I can tell, he opens the door to let the herd of elephants in and they rearrange the furniture, play a rockin' rendition of "Smells Like Teen Spirit" and skin a cat. He finishes his morning ritual off by coming into the room, tiptoeing, of course, kisses me on the forehead and tells me he's going to look for big racks.

Be jealous ladies...be very jealous.

· ○ ◐ ● ◑ ○ ·

As I made my way past the felines and the furniture to the facilities at 2 a.m., I stopped and peeked out the window...then it hit me...

He has "trained" me to look for deer in the yard... like an old dog picking up a scent, he has trained me...this may explain the overwhelming urge I have to chase the squirrel in the back yard that I've been watching for the last half hour...

Mike and I were walking through the many shops in Eureka Springs over the weekend. It was extremely crowded and we were also looking for a place to eat while doing a little window shopping.

Twice I turned to say something to him to find it wasn't him, he was off looking at something. I gave him a small speech like you would a five-year-old to stay with me in the store and hold my hand.

He agreed.

Wel-l-l...that lasted about five minutes. We were headed down the sidewalk and I spotted a place he had mentioned he wanted to eat. I reached down and grabbed his hand, leading him that way.

I turned and said, "How about we eat here?"

The man I was holding, obviously not Mike, turned to his wife, who was holding his other hand and said, "I'm going to go eat here with this lady."

She looked at me and said, "Finally some peace and quiet...just have him back by ten."

Stunned and embarrassed, I quickly released my death grip on the man's hand, looked at them both, grinned and said, "Okay, but you're buying."

I feel we bonded...

Mike is cooking breakfast and insists on watching *The Rifleman*.

I think he feels it counteracts the girlie aspect of making heart shaped waffles...

· ○ ◐ ● ◐ ○ ·

I came home to find the Spousal Unit in bed sick! This worries me on several levels...

1) For him to actually be sick enough to be in bed, I fear his days are numbered.
2) Demon Cat won't leave his side which is never a good sign...and
3) What am I going to eat?

The grief is overwhelming...

· ○ ◐ ● ◐ ○ ·

Mike had me send his new phone a photo of me so he could set it as my ring ID when I called.

Just for fun, I sent him a picture of my butt.

About ten minutes later, he received a text from AT&T that said he had used 85% of his data intake...

Hmmmm...

As I listened to the Spousal Unit explain in great detail how to hook a U haul to my Jeep, I had eerie flashbacks to Wednesday Night Gun TV Lessons...just like then, I pointed at various things and nodded at all the intense moments of him explaining wiring instructions and proper ball size to me...after the riveting 45 minute tutorial I got in the Jeep feeling somewhat more intelligent and a tad bit cocky that I had mastered this task and Mike was impressed.

He then looked at me and said, "Okay...now take the Jeep out of Overdrive."

"We have Overdrive?" was my response...it was at that moment I feel he died a little inside...

· ∘ ◦ ● ◦ ∘ ·

Last night we were lying in bed...the Spousal Unit reading a Hot Rod magazine while I solved word math problems in my head.

At one point he turned to me and asked..."Do you think the Chevy small block blah blah transmission blah blah ratio blah blah blah or do you prefer the blah blah blah blah blah?"

I gave him the 'Where is Overdrive' look and said, "Are you high?"

I shall check his pockets and underwear drawer for drugs when he goes to shower...

I heard a noise on the porch last night...I nudged the Spousal Unit several times to no avail. I determined from his snores, I was on my own.

I made my way to the living room, in the dark, hoping to catch a glimpse of the beast. As I glared between the panes of stained glass on the door, all I could see was the reflection of my nose which looks like a giants nose in the stained glass...hehehe...anyway...

So I find myself alone...in the dark...with a giant nose...and only one thing left to do...I turned on the porch light...subtle yet effective...then I watched the raccoon scurry off the porch...

Yes, I used a light switch and I'm not afraid to use it again...

Beware creatures of the night...Beware...

I have discovered the two words that make my husband melt—Harbor Freight!

Last night Mike was watching TV and made the announcement, "The older I get, the more attractive I find older women...

Silence...

"I mean, older women, but not you...

Silence...

"Because you're not old, you are young...

Silence...

"But you are still attractive; even at your age...I am not going to recover from this, am I?"

I suspect there will be a gift when I return home tonight.

* * * ● * * *

MIKE: Dang it, I just got hog jowl grease on my Ruger t-shirt."

How redneck is my husband?

* * * ● * * *

ME: You need anything from town?
MIKE: Yes, you told me last night to remind you to get something.
ME: What was it? I'll write it on my list.
MIKE: I don't remember.

I feel we may need to work on our system...

Mike opened the front door and said, "Look, this snow is just getting worse. Stay put for a little while and see what happens." Then he added, "You may be cooking your own supper tonight if I have to stay out."

I sadly nodded as I made sure he had snacks, extra socks, coveralls, charged phone, etc., and told him I had thought that through when buying groceries yesterday and purchased things I could cook too.

He glanced toward the fridge and said, "I saw a whole chicken in there. Feeling pretty confident, aren't you?"

I always sensed poultry would be my downfall...

I sometimes find misplaced "manly objects" in odd spots throughout the house...a pistol lying in bed, a hunting magazine in my underwear drawer, and even from time to time I find the toilet seat up.

I suspect this is The Spousal Unit's feeble attempt at marking his territory...Amateur...

Going to photograph a wedding Saturday evening to help out a friend, I smiled real big, brushed up against Mike and asked him if he wanted to go.

He said, "Are you kidding? I didn't even want to go to my own wedding."

I hope he can hear his alarm from the couch...

Watching *The Dugger's* on *Say Yes to the Dress:*

Mike: Is that the people with the 72 kids?
Steph: Nineteen, but yes.
Mike: And they aren't married?
Steph: Yes...they are renewing their vows.
Mike: When Jana wakes up in the morning and I'm still there...she can consider her vows renewed.

Mike just grabbed his gun and said, "I gotta go kill a squirrel for lunch before the storm hits."

I feel as if I should go free the horses from the corral and help Pa chop wood...just to help us through this...

I started carrying a different purse and caught Mike looking at it.

I said, "You like?"

He said, "That may be the ugliest thing I have ever seen."

I told him not to hold back, to tell me how he really felt.

He said, "Well, it's not as bad as the shoes you wore yesterday."

It's getting kind of cold to sleep outside, don't you think?

I got a stack of the *Stars* magazine yesterday to send to my sisters, give to Mom and for Mike. Got home from work and gave him one, but he had to shower so he could read it later—he said.

Got back from eating and he had to go to the "study"...perfect opportunity to read it...or so I thought. Apparently there is an unspoken bathroom rule that you have to read "manly" articles. (Don't even get me started on that.) Anyway, he finally got around, got ready for bed, grabbed the magazine and hit the sheets.

About half an hour later, I asked him what he thought...

"Well, I'm looking at the pictures now."

"Overjoyed, I said, "Yay...do you like them?"

From the bedroom, I heard, "No, I'm looking at the Taekwondo Tournament photos. I graduated with the Hagar Sisters..."

I feel I am narrowing down my target audience...

I wanted to share a story of the lengths of "True Love" on this special day.

I was having to work late, but Mom needed some Cokes at Elmcroft. I wasn't going to make it out there early enough, so I called Mike to do the deed.

He answered the phone and I said, "I know you are going to hate to do this, but please, I need you to go to Wal Mart (he hates going to Wal Mart) and get Mom some Cokes and take them to her at Elmcroft."

I was puzzled at the relief in his voice when he said, "Okay, okay, I thought you were going to ask me to go to "The Womanly Wall," and I was going to have to tell you no..."

Hmmmm...apparently friends, "The Womanly Wall" is the limit to our true love.

We shall test this conclusion at a later date...

Our hotel room's heat and air system has a tag on it that says it senses when you are not in the room and shuts itself off to save energy. This both baffles and fascinates Mike. Last night I came out of the bathroom to find him covered up in the bed like a mummy with just his eyes showing.

He said, "Get in the bed and be still, we're gonna make the AC shut off."

We live such exciting lives...

132

With

Child...

Steph was trying to explain the clarity and the advantages to having a Blu Ray player, High-definition television, Plasma something and blah-blah-blah...the whole "high tech gadget" bonanza is lost on me. I'm blind enough, all that fru fru tech stuff doesn't make a difference. Well...lookey there...it seems I have found the silver lining in the demeaning cloud of getting old...

STEPH: We got new neighbors last night and now every room of our apartment smells strongly of pot. Great. Lovely.
ME: Well, You should have rested well and woke up wanting a hearty breakfast.
STEPH: Funnily enough, I slept better than I have in weeks...

My daughter just asked who Bob Segar is...
Does anyone have a place she can stay tonight?

Although I'm very very very sad that the children are leaving today and they will be extremely missed (insert tear), I do have to admit sitting in the living room pantless watching TV has also been extremely missed...

STEPH:	You aren't going to wear that "out," are you?
ME:	What's wrong with it?
STEPH:	It's a bit casual for a public event.
ME:	I'm going to Wal Mart.
STEPH:	Try again.
ME:	(after changing) How is this?
STEPH:	Very sparkly holiday like. Yes! You can wear that.
ME:	Does it match my furry boots?
STEPH:	Nothing matches your furry boots, Mom.

I kinda miss Mike's generic answer of "You look fine." Ignorance is bliss...

· ∘ ◉◉●◉∘ ∘ ·

Steph: We need coal and a carrot for our snowman.
Me: You making one for pictures?
Steph: No, for Mike to shoot...

I've never been so proud..

· ∘ ◉◉●◉∘ ∘ ·

My daughter just walked out the front door and said, "I just need a minute with nature...

My child is making butter today. Yes...from cream...by hand...making butter. I'm thinking wearing pants may be my big accomplishment of the day...

SAFETY TIP #32.... When casually saying "I have lost my child," in a crowded store, Be sure to get out that she is twenty-three BEFORE they issue a "pink alert"...

My daughter just reminded me that she called me this morning at two a.m. to tell me they had been evacuated from their apartment due to all the fire alarms going off.

I apparently told her to call me back if it was a real fire. I will be checking my mail for that "Mother of the Year" award I'm sure I will receive...

My son-in-law just brought me a plate with his homemade cut up the apples, cooked his own caramel, made everything from scratch caramel apple pie and his homemade cut the pumpkin up, scoop out the guts, made a shortbread crust from scratch pumpkin cheesecake. I always dreamed my daughter would marry a man like this...

Watching TV last night and a *Flicka* movie preview came on...

STEPH: They are still making *Flicka* movies?
ME: Yes, it's like *Land Before Time*, they made like 72 of those.
STEPH: Well you know this horse will eventually have to die...Just like the dinosaurs...

And that is why my child never babysits...

○ ○ ◐ ○ ○

STEPH: I need to tell you something I'm ashamed of.
ME: Is it that you like Taylor Swift?
STEPH: Uh....No?
ME: Oh yeah...That's why I'M ashamed of you...

○ ○ ◐ ○ ○

Put on my dress to wear to Steph's shower and asked her how I looked.

She said, "Very Bohemian and hip...plus if anyone fun dies, you are all set."

Still trying to process if that was a compliment or not...

I'm frying bacon and Steph is doing Yoga...sometimes I wonder if she is really mine...

My child brought me some hand-me-downs and was explaining..."This sweater is for cocoa by the fire and this blouse is for showing property with confidence."

I picked up a shiny black low cut tank with feathers and sparkles and asked what this was for.

She said, "This is for when Mike dumps you for a trophy wife and you have to spend your nights in clubs trying to snag another man that will put up with your OCD and abnormal family."

It is comforting to see the high hopes she has for me...

Steph and Kyle are coming home next weekend and we were texting about it. This was one of her texts...

"And we are also bringing pumpkins to either shoot or throw off something."

I admit...I got a little teary eyed with how she resembles Mike in so many ways...

The other day Steph got out of the shower to a smoke filled apartment. She called Mike and they determined it was because she had turned on the heat for the first time and that all would be fine.

I got to thinking...she called Mike and not me, so I pondered on who she calls for what occasion. She calls Mike for advice on how to cook something, fix something mechanical, cut a board to build something, when her car is making a noise and for various questions on history, animals and growing things.

She calls me when something hurts or if she is people watching and wants to make fun of someone. I'd say our roles in this family have been determined and well assigned...

• ◦ ● ◐ ● ◦ •

My daughter just started a sentence with..."You know when you run babies into stuff?"

Does anyone else find this disturbing?

• ◦ ● ◐ ● ◦ •

My daughter informed me she organized the fridge today...there is a fresh food section, meat section, condiments section, crap she hates section and things that aren't good for me section...guess that about sums it up...

Last night Steph and I were going through my closet.

I pulled out a sweater and asked, "How about this?"

She said, "Sure...if you are going hiking or to the ninth season of *Friends*."

Maybe if had 2 children, the other would have been sweet...

○ ○ ◐ ◑ ○ ○

STEPH:	Guy here in bookstore giving me weird vibe. Like he might attack someone, but I feel wrong postulating that.
ME:	Postulating?
STEPH:	Figuring...thinking...
ME:	Well, just don't attack first.
STEPH:	Only weapon I have is a cell phone
ME:	You will need that cell phone to call police while running away. Can you fashion some type of shank out of your headband?
STEPH:	No, but I have razor sharp nails, they grow in naturally to a point.
ME:	Good plan.
STEPH:	The man bought a book and coffee and left. I was too quick to judge.
ME:	It happens to all of us...

I feel there were many lessons learned here today...

You would think my child was three instead of twenty-three as many times as I had to say, "Put down the baby Jesus" this weekend...

· ◦ ◐ ◉ ◐ ◦ ·

Random statement from my child during supper..."I would give you my kidney, if you needed it and I was a match."

Wow...And I was just going to ask her to do the dishes...

· ◦ ◐ ◉ ◐ ◦ ·

I'm not for sure how the events transpired last night, but around midnight, I received a text from Steph about a convict loose in their area...I guess the fact of me telling her to get a bat and go back to bed didn't set too well, because this was my text this morning...

"Goodnight, I suppose. But tomorrow you need to get that overprotective Mom gene checked out. I think yours is broken."

For the person or possum that pranced across the porch last night startling my child, which in turn, provoked my child to wake me at 2 a.m...

Did you happen to pass the shooting range in the yard on your way to the porch? You get what that is used for, right?

After receiving a picture of a bloody finger from my child and a text that said:

STEPH: Be careful when washing dishes.
ME: OMG, did you cut yourself?
STEPH: No, got shivved by the neighbor.
ME: Do you need stitches?
STEPH: I thought it might, but it's okay. Kinda cool in that I felt proud of myself for not crying and for staying calm if I had needed stitches. But it was even cooler that I didn't have to get up, put on clothes and go to a doctor.

The important part was NOT that she didn't need stitches...it was that she didn't need clothes.

FROM MY CHILD:

Juice of the poppy...> opium...> morphine...> heroin
Juice of cane...> molasses...> brown sugar...> white sugar...
Because I love you.

· ⁖ ∘●◯∘ ∘ ·

STEPH: I dreamt we were in a suburban neighborhood, but all the roads were made of water, big pools of it, and the culs-de-sac all were swimming pools.
ME: Glad you can swim.
STEPH: Also, I have been waiting 4 years to naturally use the plural for of cul-de-sac in conversation and today it finally arrived. God bless my watery dream.

· ⁖ ∘●◯∘ ∘ ·

I received two texts about a minute apart from my child last night:

1) Can you get rabies without being bitten?
2) Did you know Mimi had lived in Los Angeles?

I'm still trying to piece together if the two are related...

Our entire day in just eight texts:

STEPH: Love you, Mom, goodnight. How was your day?

ME: Good. Busy. Two closings. Sold some land. Love you too.

STEPH: Excellent. I watched a baby be born on TV. It was disgusting!

ME: I watched American Idol. It was just as scary.

STEPH: Enterprise charged us $51.60. Brazen hussies.

ME: Okay, I will call tomorrow. I can't believe I forgot to watch the birth.

STEPH: Thirteen people have died in Arkansas this year alone. Please, please be safe. You like people and talk to them in person. Be. Safe.

ME: pause...

STEPH: From the flu I mean. Loads of people have died from other things. Avoid that too.

∘ ∘ ● ● ∘ ∘ ∘

I was telling Steph about my comparison of *Finding Bigfoot* and *Gilligan's Island* and she said, "I've never seen *Gilligan's Island.*" I feel I have failed as a mother...

About the time Steph and Kyle started to leave last night, Mike noticed a nail in her tire. He and Kyle patched it while Steph and I packed their cooler with groceries and packed up all their belongings to head back on their five-hour trip. When everyone ended up back in the house saying their goodbyes, I gave them the be careful, wear your seatbelt, watch for squatches throwing rocks and don't pick up ax murderers speech.

Mike gave them a can of Fix-a-Flat just in case.

I told them if they had an accident and got stranded in the woods, they could last several days on all the food in the cooler and told them to be sure and eat the raw chicken last. I also told them if they were going to get help, to tie clothing to trees to find their way back.

Steph added..."Yeah, I hear leaving bread crumbs doesn't work very well."

Mike who had been silent up until now, said, "You can make wine with bread and fruit in the back of your toilet."

I feel we have now prepared our children for being stranded in the woods or Cell Block C...

Steph and Kyle have the opportunity to move into a farm house in Fayetteville, complete with garden spot, cheaper rent and big pond. Mike and I were discussing if they happened to get a pet and had to move for any reason, if the pet would end up with us.

Steph said, "We are getting chickens and if we move there is an easy solution. They might end up with you in a way..."

⚬ ⚬ ◐ ● ◑ ⚬ ⚬

Text while watching the Bachelor...

STEPH: Thank you for raising me the way you did so I didn't come out like a pouty little girl when I was an adult. And thank you for always finding money to buy me books. I owe you so much for that.

ME: Well, you can make a fortune later in life and put me up in a nice home with a chaffer.

STEPH: Do you mean a chauffeur? Because...to chaffer is to haggle and barter. Do you need a live-in chaffer.

ME: Yes, yes I do.

STEPH: Well, I won't be able to afford a chauffeur, but I will drive you everywhere.

ME: See, we do need a chaffer to bargain for the chauffeur.

STEPH: silence...

Demon Cat
and Tuesday

For those of you that don't have pets you may not understand this, but just like children, pets develop personalities. Cats, dogs, turtles, horses, whatever...they grow on you and have a distinct way of acting.

Take Tuesday...she is flat out a little hussy trollop who loves no one but her human, Mike. Demon Cat, on the other hand, is mischievous, comical, playful and loyal to no one. He does have his moments of sweetness though.

Like this morning, I had hit the snooze one too many times and he was ready for his morning treat. He so gently got on the bed, walked up and patted his little paw on my cheek as to say, "Good morning my dear sweet human, have you forgotten something?"

Precious, I tell you! It was followed up by him sneezing in my face, but I'm sure that was just an unfortunate coincidence. I hear in some cultures, it's even good luck...can someone get me a tissue?

Demon Cat has picked a new sleeping spot right at my feet. This morning I rolled over, stretched and inadvertently launched the ferocious feline airborne across the room...I swear I heard Tuesday snicker...when he makes his debut from hiding under the bed, I will report on his condition...

My neighbor has like 72 cats...a few of them came a'calling last night. Demon Cat seemed to think he was up for the task...poor neutered little ball of fur, all he could do was stand at the window and howl...ALL NIGHT.

I am now looking for a sacrifice, a stud cat of some sort to shut up the howling hussy's tonight...any takers?

* * * * * * *

Demon Cat and Tuesday have grown accustomed to a cat-treat when I get up for my coffee in the morning. IF for some reason I try to sleep in or hit the snooze one too many times, they become a bit antsy and try to urge me to get up. Demon Cat will look for any part of my body not covered and just bite it...I have learned to expect this. Tuesday on the other hand is a sly little hussy who quietly just sits...on my bladder...she is diabolical, I tell you...

* * * * * * *

Having my morning coffee with Demon Cat, Tuesday and Wonder Woman...I'm watching the cats swat the windows at the birds feeding outside...occasionally seeing Demon Cat run smack dab into the glass, really wanting them, but coming to the bitter reality that he can't have them.

I suspect this is comparable to The Spousal Unit and me walking past a shoe store or ice cream parlor...I feel your pain DC, I feel your pain...

I have discovered my Jeep takes on the faint odor of cat urine when it rains...

This both mystifies and disturbs me...

As my face powder hit the floor and the last of it spilled out, I didn't hesitate at all dropping to my knees to soak up the last bit I needed...

I did not, however, anticipate Demon Cat taking this as a time to play and rolling over in my small pile.

As I watched my last bit of face powder walk off attached to his fur I realized...I do have limits...I will not powder my face with a Demon Cat...so if I seem a bit shiny today, please forgive me, but no...I didn't go there...

I am amazed at the lengths Demon Cat will go to gain access to the ornaments on the tree. He's like the Macgyver of felines. Yet he still crashes into closed windows chasing a bird outside...

Last night I dreamed I was riding in one of those racing boats that go way too fast for my liking. The seatbelt was so tight I could barely breathe. I woke up and Demon Cat was sitting on my chest looking at me...which came first the cat or the dream?

· • •⬤• • ·

Had my alarm set for 6:10, woke up at 5:55 and then dozed back off...dreamed I was sitting outside at a beautiful table with my dad, Steph and Albert Pujols...I don't even follow football...

Anyway, we were having deer meat. Then Demon Cat jumped on my chest and woke me up, which in turn caused me to sit straight up and knock the glass of water off my nightstand, which in turn caused Demon Cat to freak, dig claws into my chest and run.

My phone then went off at 6:06 with a counteroffer text. Got up and came to turn on TV and hit the "Input" button about 6:10...why is that button even there?

This may have been the most trying 15 minutes of my life...

Yeah, it's all fun and games until the cat realizes the moth landed on your knee...and you didn't...

• ○ ◐ ● ○ ○ •

Mike walked in the bathroom to kiss me goodbye. Tuesday, the cat, walked up between us and dropped to the ground, stretching out and purring.

He halted the kiss, bent over to rub her belly and patted her head.

I'd almost swear I saw her look back at me and laugh...

Hussy.

• ○ ◐ ● ○ ○ •

Let me tell you...the first time you have to pull a piece of tinsel out of your pet's derriere...your whole decorating scheme changes...

• ○ ◐ ● ○ ○ •

I walked in the bedroom and went to pet Demon Cat who was curled up at the foot of my bed...

The Spousal Unit was watching...turns out it was not the cat, it was my black bra.

I don't know that Mike has ever looked at me with such pity before...

Tuesday and Demon Cat are sticking close. This is normally a sign of impending doom.

Possibly, I'm than I think, or the storms coming are going to be bad...

Either way, I'm bummed...I really wanted to watch the new *Cupcake Wars* tonight...

The incident occurred at approximately 3:35 a.m. when one Jana Caldwell was making her way to the facilities in the dark. From information gathered at the scene, it appears the belt on her robe dragging along the floor provoked some type of animal attack, around and about the victim's ankle area. Authorities are leaning towards Demon Cat as the perpetrator, but said victim has identified her attacker as a Squatch.

More details to follow after further investigating...

I'm going to speak to you about something that is inevitable if you own a pet. At some point in your life together, whether it's when you wake up confused one night, when you stumble to the restroom in the dark or when you are still on a post surgery high...you will mistakenly pet the wrong end of your furry friend. That's all I have to say about that...

I'm going to say this once...and we are never to speak of it again...when blindly making your way from the bedroom to the bathroom in the middle of the night...always...and I mean ALWAYS check to confirm there is no cat drinking from the toilet before you sit down...always...

If you knew my family,

You would understand...

Walked in to pick up my mother yesterday and she had another company's Real Estate Catalog...

ME: Why do you have that catalog Mom?

MOM: Because you work there.

ME: No Mom, I work at Carter City & County Realty.

MOM: But your picture is in this one, you used to work there.

ME: Nope, I have never worked there.
        She turns to the man beside her and says, "I guess that's not her picture in there."

MOM: But we have picked out a couple of farms we want.

ME: Okay, but you have to buy them through me.

MOM: We'll see...

It's good to know I always have my family...

· ∘ ◦ ● ◦ ∘ ·

Still sitting in Cardiologist office after two Starbucks is not an easy task...lots of old people in here...I take that as a good sign for Mom...

ME: Mom, I'm going to pick you up in a couple of hours to take you out to eat and shop a little for Mother's Day.

MOM: Now? Well crap, guess I have to shower and blow dry my hair. Not just me and you? Stephanie is going, isn't she?

It's the tender moments like this I will cherish always...

· ○ ◐●◑ ○ ·

As I sit in my lonely corner listening to La Madre snore off her happy juice while watching all the staff working and using large medical words that I just nod and pretend to understand...I ponder...

You think if I score some scrubs and latex gloves they will let me operate on someone? Nothing major, just an appendix or tonsil or something.

· ○ ◐●◑ ○ ·

Mom's awake and according to the Smiley Face Pain Chart on the wall, she is five-six=hurts even more...

The nice nurse in pink named Crystal just gave her pills to fix that—

We like Crystal...

Mom lying on the couch and out of the blue, just asked, "What's a four-letter word for breast milk?"
We may need to adjust her meds...

Have collected La Madre from La Airport Terminal...she left her meds in Texas, lost her scarf somewhere between Texas and Arkansas and her luggage is tagged with yellow police tape, which has yet to be explained...yep...things seem back to normal.

Yesterday mom and I stopped in Searcy to eat on our way back. Ordered an appetizer and we were dining on it when the waitress brought us our entrees in "TO GO" containers...I hadn't realized my dining reputation had made it that far south...

Trying to explain to my mother..."Yes, it's a real book...no, I'm not quitting my day job...no, they didn't pay me up front... and...yes, if I have my picture made again, I will wear a Spanx..."
I'm going home now to nap...in the fetal position...

Mama told me there'd be days like this...actually no, she didn't. I'm finding I was not properly prepared for many of life's little surprises...I'm guessing that the whole Santa Claus/Easter Bunny thing is a scam too?

· ○ ◉ ● ◉ ○ ·

Taking parental unit to the center for transportation by air in the period after twelve noon and before sunset...it shall be a magical adventure...

· ○ ◉ ● ◉ ○ ·

Busy and late day at work yesterday so Mike came by the office and we decided to eat at El Acupulco.

Enjoyed a great meal and were visiting with some friends discussing real estate, food, and nuclear fusion as the holy grail of energy sources when it hit me...the Parental Unit was at my house waiting on supper... Ooops...and I wonder why no one ever asks me to watch their kids...

Conversation with my niece:

ZOE: Yeah, we are reading this book for English and it took place during the war and the guy gets hurt "down there" and he falls in love with a woman he can never be with because she is like a hooker or something. Her name was Lady Brett Ashley...

Dang...all we ever read in school was *White Fang*...

As I waited for my appointment and watched the kids play "keep away" in the yard next door, it took me back to my childhood. I can remember my sisters playing that game with me. It was such a special time when my big sisters took time to play those fun games with me...it just meant so much.

However...

The more I studied this "game," the more I realized they weren't playing with me, they were playing pitch...I was just running around in circles.

I suspect "play time" with my siblings is what has led to my Social Dysfunction...as well as my keen athletic ability...

In June 2000, my sisters and I took part in a "Sibling Study" in Houston. My dad had Alpha 1 Antitrypsin Deficiency and we were all being tested to see if we did. My niece, Sydney, was just a baby and we were taking turns holding her in the waiting room while the other two sisters were getting blood drawn. Jeania was back getting probed and prodded and I was walking around with the baby waiting on them.

When she finished, she walked back in and I looked at her, still holding Syd, and said, "So, now what?"

Without missing a beat, she said, "Well, now we wait for the results to see who your baby daddy is," and walked off.

This caught the attention of the entire room who up until now had been dormant. As I scanned the room with that "deer in the headlight" look, I realized I didn't stand a chance of explaining myself, so I picked up the diaper bag, kissed the baby on the forehead and said, "All righty, then," and walked out like I owned the place.

Fast forward to 2005 and Jeania's 40th birthday...

A four hundred pound female impersonator in a hula skirt and coconut bra sent to her office...all for her dancing pleasure...

I'd say we're even now...

Left my grocery list on the counter for everyone to add what they needed to it. Got to Wal Mart and these were the last four items on my list...Joy & Happiness...Peace on Earth...Good Will Towards Men...charcoal starter...

This family just ain't right...

Waiting on my 1:00 showing. I'm in my tennis shoes, I haven't bathed and I'm pretty sure I just discovered chocolate gravy in my hair. Luckily my clients are family and professionalism is optional...

Pain Chart
#2

Hurts a Little...

Jana Caldwell:

1) Tylenol PM=Restful night's sleep
2) Tylenol PM=Coma

• ◦ ◦●◦ ◦ •

I fought the couch and the couch won...and during the scuffle, I pulled a little something 'round back. Gave up "walking the soreness out," after a week and went to the Doc yesterday. She gave me a shot to loosen things up and sent me home for the afternoon to sleep it off. I called the Spousal Unit and he picked me up and drove me home.

By the time I got home, I was starting to feel no pain. I was standing in the bedroom trying to get undressed when I touched the spot where I got the shot.

I felt what I thought was a big fluffy bandage.

Upon further investigating, I pulled a fabric softener sheet out of my undies.

So, I'm standing there, half dressed, half drunk and laughing uncontrollably at the thought of whether the nurse that gave me the shot thought the fabric softener sheet was actually a fabric softener sheet or that I was wearing a diaper...

Not as funny since the fog has lifted this morning...

Yesterday when I went to see the doc, my pulseox (new word) was low so they did a chest x-ray.

When I stepped in the room, the sweet little girl told me I could leave my shirt on, but needed to remove my bra and nametag.

My first instinct was to say, "If I had a nickel..." but I refrained. Anyway...I got the nametag off and thought, this is a snap. I started by slipping my arm back in my shirt, piece of cake. Slipped that strap off and proceeded to try to slip my other arm out. Bad choice. Upon further review I figured out okay...put the empty arm back first and the other should just slide out...or one would think. My left arm had apparently claimed its independence and refused to go back in the sleeve. Fine...embrace your freedom and I will remove my right arm. It occurred to me I had been at this for a good 5 minutes while the little girl was standing by patiently.

I could only imagine I looked like one of those inflatable Santa's in a wind storm...arms flopping around. Poor kid...probably ruined her whole child-like dream of the jolly fat guy. I then rapidly took my shirt off, removed my bra, put my shirt back on and told her I was ready.

It may have taken a toll to get to that photo, but I tell you what...I passed that x-ray in the hall on that light board they display them on and I tell you what...I looked goooooood! Tall...thin...tan...

Thinking of asking for a copy for my profile pic...

So when the nurse said Decadron may keep me awake tonight...she was right. I'm making shadow puppets on the ceiling with the light from my cell phone...

Isn't technology grand?

I forgot my purse in the Dr. office and had to go back into the room...they should really mark those better...and just for future reference men...if you are going to be undressing...pull the door to...just sayin'...

After a little scare with my heart...

Waiting on an MRI and they are making me take a pill...okay...I took it...nothing yet.

Diazepam.....sounds made up to me...

Mike gave me coffee, sat me in a chair and told me not to talk to anyone.

I hope he comes back.

Okay, so tomorrow is my last heart test. They gave me Valium to take 30 minutes beforehand. The last time they did that, I woke up the next morning in my underwear and Mike had a weird grin all day...now he just keeps looking at me and winking.

⋅ ◦ ◉ ◉ ◦ ⋅

After a sleepless night, 4 doses of medicine, several drug induced incidents I can't even remember and 72 tissues scattered throughout the bedroom...for me...Mike wakes up in a sickeningly cheery mood and said, "It's going to be a beautiful day out. How do you feel?"

If the look on my face was not enough to tell the tale, I said, "Well, now I can't breathe at all, my throat is killing me, and as a new development for the night, now my eyes won't stop watering."

Feeling he'd lost this conversation with nothing to say to make me feel better or gain ground, he said, "You hungry?"

I like a man who thinks quickly on his feet...

I'm not happy. The ENT says the lung Dr. is wrong. He says that the uvula is not the problem. He is setting up an appointment to look for cancer in the esophagus and sending me to a heart doctor.

He said he has ruled out everything else and now he is checking for more serious.

Something about a rare bird and a coughing dog.

I really need to start bringing someone with me...

      • ◦ ◦ ● ◦ ◦ •

About to get the happy drugs...things are looking up... oh...pretty spots....

      • ◦ ◦ ● ◦ ◦ •

Went to the doctor this week and found out I had lost eleven pounds in the last three months. I attribute my weight loss to my avoidance of daily scheduled exercise, my viewing "diet" as a four-letter-word, and my overwhelming addiction to pudding cups...

I find this combination works well and plan to celebrate with a coffee and apple tart...

See, I eat fruit...

I am having a little trouble kicking this Bronchitis, so I went back to the doctor yesterday to get a shot. While I was waiting in the little room, not going through the drawers, I was casually scanning all the books and pamphlets on the counter.

In my own little warped world, I found it quite humorous there was a brochure on Chronic Idiopathic Constipation...right beside the book *The Little Engine That Could.*

While I pictured the doctor giving a patient both these books to take home for studying, I got to laughing so hard that I might have wet myself just a tiny bit...

I did not, however, find the pamphlet for that...

I have developed a small quarter size rash on my ankle. I realize I was wading thru brush and debris all weekend but I am not allergic to poison ivy so I am convinced it is the flesh eating disease I saw on the news...

I fear this will deeply impact swimsuit season...

Was trying to explain the monitor, what it involved and what it was supposed to do to Barry...

Barry: So that thing around your neck is hooked to that thing in your throat?

Me: Well, sorta. It keeps track of my acid levels in my stomach.

Barry: How big is it?

Me: According to Google, smaller than a hen egg.

Barry: So do they go back in and take it out?

Me: Well, not really. I pass it.

Barry: So you just $&@% it out?

Me: Well, in so many words, yes.

Barry: Cool. Bring it in when you get it back so we can see it.

I can safely say I have reached "one of the guys" status in our office...

∘ ∘ ◑◐ ∘ ∘

People watching in the Cardiology Dept. is really not as thrilling as you would think...

∘ ∘ ◑◐ ∘ ∘

Okay...strip down, cover yourself in gel and run on this treadmill... I mean it's not the worst date I've been on but come on... Seriously?

Thinks she feels better and is looking forward to work before Drs. tomorrow afternoon and thanks everyone for all their sweet thoughts and thinks that pudding should be its own food group...yeah that 'bout covers it for now...

Last night I had my head propped up in bed so I could breathe. My head slipped off the pillow and hit the metal headboard. I told Mike, "This is the third time today I've hit my head and when I do, my teeth hurt. Am I having teeth problems, too? Look, when I do this (tapping the back of my head against the headboard) it hurts!"

He told me not to worry that it was just sinus pressure and I was feeling it in my teeth.

Satisfied with this explanation and convinced I wasn't going to be toothless; I relaxed against the headboard again.

"Now," he said. "Do you normally hit your head that many times a day?"

Thinking back on the events of the day, I said, "More than one would think, yes."

He nodded and said, "Makes sense now."

I don't know what he's getting at...

I need to set a scene for this story...Picture a dark hospital room...2am...Pleasantly relaxed with Morphine...Enter a Medical Professional...And in place of the female anatomy word she was using let's just call it an "Easter Bunny"...

MED PRO: Good Morning, How are we feeling today?

ME: I'm good...little sore

MED PRO: That's to be expected. I'm here to remove your Catheter..

ME: Puzzled...I..Don't...Have One?

MED PRO: Yes ma'am, you do.

ME: Morphine high & puzzled...I'm pretty sure it's gone because I have been going to the bathroom...Although it is a little difficult at times... Why is it? Why is it difficult to go to the bathroom?

MED PRO: That's because they packed your "Easter Bunny."

ME: Blank Stare... I'm sorry they did what to my "Easter Bunny"?

MED PRO: They pack your "Easter Bunny" in surgeries like this.

ME: What does my "Easter Bunny" have to do with my Esophagus?

MED PRO: Well not much..

ME: Okay...I'm lost. They fixed my Esophagus...Why would they even be in the neighborhood of my "Easter Bunny"?

MED PRO: Looking at her chart....You had a

	hysterectomy, right?
ME:	Ummm...Nope.
MED PRO:	It's early...I'm sorry. You are fine. It's
	early. We don't have to pack anything...
ME:	Good to know...

I never saw that MED PRO again but the next little girl that came in to check on me later chuckled and asked..."How's your "Easter Bunny"?

· ○ ◉ ◉ ◉ ◑ ○ ·

I was standing in the bathroom looking at my scars from last week. There are 5 of them scattered among my abdomen along with one from 10 years ago for my gallbladder. If I suck in and squint really hard the arrangement resembles washboard abs... Of course if you just look at them like they are they resemble gunshot wounds. I haven't decided yet which story to go with during swimsuit season.... I suspect the latter may be more fun...

I make my coffee, not because I can drink it but because it makes me feel normal...Last night I wore myself out just retrieving my checkbook from my purse...The only noticeable improvement I can see is I'm now allowed to go to the bathroom alone.... Color me tired of sitting and grouchy.

• ∘ ◦ ● ◦ ∘ •

I have had a terrible, painful, embarrassing, chronic cough for at least 5 years..I couldn't tell you the last peaceful nights sleep I or Mike have had. But....Since the surgery I have not coughed one time! I am truly blown away by this. Aside from the fact that it feels like someone beat my torso with a baseball bat, I am a new woman! A very grateful, lucky, new woman.

Cooking

Tips...

COOKING TIP #14...Pampered Chef cooking stones stay hot loooooooooong after the food is removed, eaten and possibly till after you are back from the ER...

COOKING TIP #24...When working with hot sugar and getting it on your finger...DO NOT put in mouth to cool off...

COOKING TIP #26...When pre-heating oven for baking a puff pastry, DO NOT lay said puff pastry on or near stove to thaw while you shower...I think you know how this ends...

COOKING TIP #36...When rinsing off the emulsion blender under the faucet, RESIST the urge to see what happens when you turn it on...at least while clothed for work...

About the Author

Jana Caldwell is an energetic forty-something wife and mother pondering the mysteries of the universe in small-town Arkansas. She makes her living as a multi-million dollar producing real-estate agent. In her spare time she is a dedicated Facebook comedienne with a following that has made this book possible. She gets a great deal of joy from the many fund raising activities and charities she is involved in. She loves spending time with her husband, daughter, and son-in-law. It is her life's dream to meet Ellen. Oh...and she is kind to animals and loves children.

jana.caldwell.10@facebook.com

CPSIA information can be obtained at www.ICGtesting.com
Printed in the USA
LVOW051908190513

334450LV00002B/2/P

9 780988 954274